Teenage Heroes
The Hero's Journey of Adolescence

Donated To The Library By

Matthew Winkler

"*Mentoring Teenage Heroes* educates and inspires adults to look at the journey of adolescents in a new light, one that acknowledges tragedy, triumph, and growth are essential in the developmental process."

—JUSTIN BENDALL,
School Counselor, The Rectory School

"Every parent, coach, and teacher should read *Mentoring Teenage Heroes*."

—ANDREW J. VADNAIS,
Head of School, South Kent School

"*Mentoring Teenage Heroes* is enticing, informative and exceedingly well written. Anyone involved with the inner life of teens can find here an accessible and invaluable resource to help them interpret what's going on in their lives."

—REV ART PURCARO OSA,
Assistant Vice President for Mission and Ministry, Villanova University

MENTORING TEENAGE HEROES

THE HERO'S JOURNEY OF ADOLESCENCE

Matthew P. Winkler

woodhall press

NORWALK - BRANFORD, CONNECTICUT

Author's Note

I have relied upon the recollections of those who were present during the events described in this book. There are no composite characters or events in this book, although some nonessential people and events have been omitted. I have changed the names of many of the people in this book and sometimes altered distinguishing details about them in order to protect their privacy.

Back cover illustration © TED Conferences LLC, designed by Kirill Yeretsky
Author photo © Matthew P. Winkler

Library of Congress Cataloging-in-Publication Data available

978-0-9975437-1-1 (paperback Amazon)
978-0-9975437-0-4 (e-book Amazon)

The author and Woodhall Press LLP assume no liability for accidents happening to, or injuries sustained by, readers who engage in the activities described in this book.

This book is written for teachers,
coaches, parents, counselors,
and mentors of all stripes

but, like them,

this book is dedicated to
the next generation: today's teenagers.

Contents

Introduction

When you were a teenager, you encountered a story—a book or movie—that infected you, got under your skin, branded you with its invisible tattoo. Your parents and teachers didn't understand you, the boy or girl of your dreams didn't notice you, but that story sure had your number. It was so disturbingly familiar—an inexplicable feeling of déjà vu.

It's a safe bet that the hero of the story was shaken from his or her ordinary life, dropped into a strange world, tested against overwhelming odds and symbolically destroyed, only to be reborn triumphant and finally return home, transformed and larger than life. This recurring cycle can be found in ancient myths of almost every culture, worldwide. James Joyce termed it the "monomyth," and comparative mythologist Joseph Campbell called it the "hero's journey." In his seminal book, *The Hero with a Thousand Faces,* Campbell argued that every hero is the same hero, merely adapted to the unique context of each culture, and he referenced dozens of examples from around the globe. This universal, mythical structure echoes throughout today's novels, films, and television shows. And it's probably what hooked you as a teenager.

You could relate to that story because it was your own story, writ large. Hadn't you been tossed, headfirst, into the choppy seas of adolescence? Weren't you struggling to navigate those uncharted waters with nothing but your own wits, a few close friends, and maybe just one mentor who "got" you? Ironically, every teenager around you was enduring a similar ordeal, undergoing his or her own personal hero's journey, following a pattern that has replayed for eons—a rite of passage as old as the myths that metaphorically describe it.

Mentoring Teenage Heroes is written for parents, teachers, coaches, and other ex-adolescents who are now guiding the new generation of teens as they tumble through fresh waves of clarity and confusion, triumph and defeat, love and heartbreak. By reviewing Campbell's original scholarship on this subject and tracing its influence on contemporary movies and books, readers will learn to identify this underlying pattern in examples as familiar as "Theseus and the Minotaur," "Cinderella," the *Star Wars* saga, the *Harry Potter* series, and *The Hunger Games* trilogy. Instead of presenting Percy Jackson and Katniss Everdeen as flavors of the week, *Mentoring Teenage Heroes* will tie them to the myths they spring from and offer insights into why these modern fictional characters resonate with today's teenagers. Unlike their matinee idols, our kids aren't at the center of dystopian or intergalactic conflicts, but they feel like they are.

Mentoring Teenage Heroes relates the true stories of Colin and Cynthia, two compelling young people on very different journeys that reveal the flexibility of the hero's journey formula: Colin's story spans two decades; Cynthia's covers five years. Colin loves his mom, but he is heartsick for his absent father. Cynthia is a gifted athlete, heading off to college on a soccer scholarship, but her illicit, secret life nearly destroys her. These two contrasting narratives propel the reader through twelve chapters and serve as a basis for understanding how the dramatic transition from childhood to adulthood is reflected in ancient myths and modern storytelling. For most adults, daily life is a routine grind. For teenagers, it's an epic struggle for identity.

Foreword

Joseph Campbell was a world-renowned expert in comparative mythology and a professor at Sarah Lawrence College for thirty-eight years. He is best known for coining the phrase "follow your bliss" and for developing the concept of the hero's journey, a universal formula that underlies all myths. Campbell published his seminal work, *The Hero with a Thousand Faces*, in 1949. As its title suggests, the book compares heroic myths from around the world, pointing out the essential elements they share.

In the 1970s a young filmmaker named George Lucas seized upon the familiar plot formula described in Campbell's book. He used the hero's journey as the framework for his *Star Wars* series, and he credits Campbell with that inspiration.[1] Books, video games, and television shows are also filled with stories that echo the ancient pattern of a hero on a physical or emotional quest that results in his or her transformation.

This would not surprise Joseph Campbell, who frequently emphasized the universal psychological underpinnings of the hero's journey formula. The reason that myths are fundamentally the same in every culture, he argued, is because all human beings share basically the same psychology. We experience every day, year, and period of our lives in similar ways, regardless of race, language, and culture. After more than fifty years of studying the subject, Campbell remained convinced that myths tell us how to live, how to be human, which is why the ancient hero's journey paradigm remains relevant in the modern world.

But what is the hero's journey, exactly? Think of it as a cycle. Imagine a circular clock with the hour hand sweeping around its face. The first three hours take place in the hero's ordinary world, from which the hero departs at three o'clock. The hero spends the next six hours in some unfamiliar, "special" world before returning home at nine o'clock. The story culminates in the hero's ordinary world during those last three hours.

Of course there's more to it than that. Campbell isolated seventeen specific points within the hero's journey. Other scholars have distilled the monomyth to just four stages or expanded it to more than two thousand. For the purposes of this book, we'll refer to twelve cardinal points.

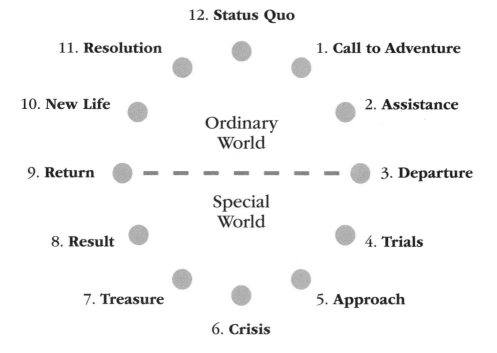

12. **Status Quo**

11. **Resolution** 1. **Call to Adventure**

10. **New Life** Ordinary World 2. **Assistance**

9. **Return** Special World 3. **Departure**

8. **Result** 4. **Trials**

7. **Treasure** 5. **Approach**

6. **Crisis**

In principle, any quest story includes these key moments in the hero's journey.

12:00 Status Quo: The equilibrium at the start of the story.
1:00 Call to Adventure: The hero receives a challenge or summons. Jack is offered magic beans in exchange for his cow. Alice sees and follows the white rabbit.
2:00 Assistance: Merlin helps Arthur; Obi-Wan Kenobi helps a young Skywalker.

3:00   Departure: The hero crosses the threshold. We're not in Kansas anymore!

4:00   Trials: The hero solves a riddle, slays a monster, escapes from a trap.

5:00   Approach: No more stalling. The hero marches out to meet his or her fate.

6:00   Crisis: The hero faces death and (symbolically) dies, only to be reborn.

7:00   Treasure: As a result, the hero claims some wisdom or material treasure.

8:00   Result: Do the monsters surrender or give chase?

9:00   Return: The hero crosses back through the barrier into his or her ordinary world.

10:00   New Life: The hero has changed and has outgrown his or her old life.

11:00   Resolution: All the plot lines get straightened out.

12:00   Status Quo: A new equilibrium has been achieved, better than the original status quo.

Consider the fairy tale "Cinderella." The ancient Greek author Herodotus mentions a similar story in his Histories, written over two thousand years ago. Indeed, more than 340 versions of "Cinderella" have been collected from as far afield as Korea, Vietnam, and the Philippines. In 1950 Walt Disney adapted a three-hundred-year-old French variant to create the well-known classic movie. Cinderella's story has endured for two millennia because it metaphorically describes the universal quest of every young lover on the cusp of adulthood, nervously yearning for the perfect partner and a new life.

Can you trace the monomyth cycle in this example? Cinderella lives a miserable life as a virtual slave to her wicked stepsisters and step-mother. Then, one day her family is invited to a royal ball. Cinderella anticipates the event but is intentionally left behind. Unexpectedly, a fairy godmother provides Cinderella with the means to attend in style. A magical coach carries Cinderella out of her ordinary world of drudgery and oppression into a special world of luxury and opportunity. She meets the prince, who might dash or fulfill all her hopes for a new life. They fall in love, but the clock strikes midnight and Cinderella flees before her enchantments expire. She resumes her life of servitude but retains the confidence she won at the ball until the prince finds her, and they live happily ever after.

This pattern is not found only in fairy tales and ancient myths. It provides the structure behind many modern stories. Consider the plot of *The Martian* by Andy Weir. This story begins with Mark Watney in the company of his fellow astronauts. When a storm develops on the Martian surface, they evacuate, leaving Mark behind due to an accident. He accepts the call to adventure, to try to survive in a hostile environment. He receives assistance from the Hab living structure and the supplies still inside it. He spends most of the story marooned on Mars, where he faces various trials. Initially he overcomes starvation by cultivating the potatoes intended for consumption, and he establishes contact with NASA. Mark's crops die when his indoor garden freezes, radically shrinking his food supplies. This is Mark's darkest hour. His fate seems certain, but he tightens his rations and sets off for the Mars Ascent Vehicle (MAV), parked at Schiaparelli Crater. He overcomes hazards to reach it and then follows instructions to deconstruct much of the MAV to make it light enough to rendezvous with his shipmates as they pass by Mars. The connection doesn't go as planned, but Mark's crewmates manage to rescue him anyway, concluding his transformative adventure. All the loose ends are tied up as Mark reflects on the importance of human community.

After you've seen the hero's journey spelled out, examples pop up everywhere. Almost every book in the Harry Potter series begins with Harry at home before departing for another year at Hogwarts and ends with him returning home for summer vacation. Think of the last book you read or the last movie you saw. Does it fit the hero's journey pattern?

Now turn that lens toward yourself. What is the status quo in your own life? When did you last leave your emotional comfort zone and make your way through unfamiliar territory, pursuing some challenge? Did you complete that quest and restore the equilibrium of your daily life? Of course you didn't slay any dragons or fight Voldemort, but didn't you overcome some obstacle? Didn't you achieve a career goal or satisfy some desire? And aren't you better for having done it?

Teenage Heroes asks exactly this question of the adolescents that we teach, coach, and mentor. Aren't they all in some stage of an epic quest? The hero's journey cycle could span a day, a sports season, or a school year. It could apply to the emotional arc of a love affair, the academic challenge of an AP course, or the multiyear voyage of adolescence itself. This book focuses on two such dramatic, high-stakes examples. Chapter by chapter, we'll follow the true stories of Colin and Cynthia, two typical kids on their own unique journeys. Along the way we'll connect their experiences to each stage of the monomyth.

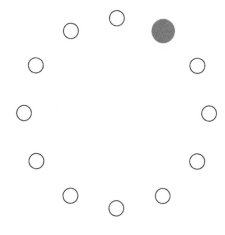

CHAPTER 1

Call to Adventure

Imagine the face of a clock with both hour and minute hands touching twelve, indicating the status quo, the normal state of things. A story begins here, introducing the hero's ordinary world. This hour of equilibrium is disrupted by the first step in our hero's journey. The clock tolls once in the distance: the Call to Adventure.

ONE O'CLOCK: **Colin's Origin Story**

Kelly lay in bed waiting for the contractions to stop. Lying on her side, she stroked the basketball of her belly and talked to her unborn son. "Settle down, Colin. Time to go to sleep." The name Colin had always been a favorite of hers, and according to her book of baby names, it meant "first son."

This was her favorite part of the day, coasting off to sleep in the silence and comfort of her lifelong home, her bedroom filled with childhood memories. She'd been having Braxton Hicks contractions for a few weeks, but they always went away when she lay down.

She'd attended her friend's baby shower earlier, so maybe Colin was reacting to the rich food.

There were moments during the party when Kelly's contractions had been so strong she had almost walked to the hospital around the corner, but that would have spoiled the baby shower. Kelly was three weeks overdue and felt like a blimp. She'd never been skinny, but this baby made her constantly hungry. And he gave her acne. But her hair grew thicker now, and more ginger than blond.

She rode home from the party with Judy, her best friend since fourth grade. For fifteen years, Kelly had spent part of every summer with Judy's family at their lakeside cabin. In one famous incident, the two girls conspired to sneak off together in a canoe. Figuring no one would notice as long as they were back before dark, they paddled out to the center of the lake. As the sun started to set, the distant shore looked the same in all directions. They hurried in a likely direction until Judy's uncle motored up in his fishing boat. He towed the miscreants back to camp, where Judy's mom scolded them and made them wash all the dishes for the rest of the trip. They had grown closer through mischief like that, and Judy was the only one who shared Kelly's darkest secret.

Their entire town knew that Kelly was pregnant at twenty by some unnamed father. That was scandalous news, and gossip stained Kelly's dad, a pillar of the community and the popular head of the high school English department. Two generations of past students still lived in their town, so everyone had a pet theory about Mr. McIntyre's "bastard grandchild." Kelly remembered when she broke the news to him and her mom five months earlier.

She sat across from them in the living room of the small, three-bedroom ranch where she'd opened presents every Christmas morning for twenty years. She felt small on the sunken corduroy cushions of the couch. The tiny figurines on the coffee table seemed to be accusing her. Her mom and dad sat in matching chairs, sturdy but a little threadbare. As usual, her dad wore a pressed shirt and matching necktie, his suit coat already hanging in the closet. Her mother's hair was cut short, barely touching the collar of her patterned blouse. They both waited, watching her through their wire-rimmed glasses.

Kelly said the words, "I'm pregnant."

A long pause.

"Have you seen a doctor?" her father asked. Her mom was silent.

"Yes."

Taking a deep breath, Kelly prayed he wouldn't ask about the father.

"Are you going to get married?" he asked.

Kelly shook her head, looked at her feet. "I was thinking about . . . adoption."

Her dad stormed out of the house. His first two kids had gone to college and done well. Kelly had flunked out after just one year. And now this. Kelly's mom held her as she cried and didn't ask any questions.

Kelly's dad came back a few hours later and wordlessly slipped a book into her hand, *Irish Baby Names*. He took something from his pocket and then opened the small clamshell box. He presented Kelly with a Claddagh ring, the traditional Irish design with a crowned heart held in two hands, typically exchanged between lovers. "Just in case anyone gives you shit."

She wore the ring on her left hand with the heart turned in, unavailable, spoken for. This was enough for strangers, but the townies still whispered beyond Mr. Mac's earshot. Who was the father? Was it her high school sweetheart? A college fling? The mystery was even deeper than they knew.

Kelly had been careful about birth control throughout her first long-term relationship, except at the very end. During what she and Judy referred to as "the lost weekend," Kelly broke up with her steady college boyfriend, then bumped into an old flame at a wild party and awoke in his bed the next morning. Eight weeks later, Kelly's first OB-GYN visit confirmed what she had feared: She was pregnant. Having slept with both men within the space of a few days, she wasn't sure who the father was, but she was too ashamed to tell anyone except Judy. Instead she resolved to handle things alone. At first she planned on adoption, but as the life grew inside her, she decided she needed this child.

And now she lay in bed, expecting the Braxton Hicks contractions to stop. But this time they didn't stop. She counted the seconds in a whisper, but the squeezes came without pattern and without the usual waves of pain. She felt an unfamiliar pressure. It didn't feel like anything described in the pregnancy books. Was her water breaking?

She got out of bed. Fluid rushed down her thighs. She turned on the light and looked down. Blood covered her legs, her feet, the floor.

"Oh my God," she said, and then a wall sealed off her emotions. *Something's wrong. Need to deal with it. Call the doctor.* She hurried to her parents' room, scarlet footprints on the carpet.

"Mom, wake up!" Kelly snapped on the light and lifted the phone off the nightstand. Her mom squinted awake, saw the blood, and sprang out of bed. Kelly dialed her doctor's number but only reached the answering service. Her mom piled towels at her feet as Kelly left a message, hot blood streaming down her legs.

"Kelly, what's wrong?" Her mom asked.

"I don't know!"

The phone rang, and Kelly snatched it.

"Hi, Kelly. This is Dr. Rubenstein. You reported some bleeding?"

"Yes."

"Okay, passing some fluid is normal. Are you passing any clots?"

"Yes, I'm passing clots."

"Alright. Are they the size of almonds or the size of walnuts?"

"Dr. Rubenstein, they're the size of grapefruits."

"Kelly, you need to get to the hospital. You need to get there immediately."

• • •

As her mom drove to the hospital, Kelly leaned out the window, puking baby-shower cake. Judy caught up to them on Route 17, panicked by Kelly's phone call. The evening fog had frozen on the roads, and Kelly's mom drove slowly over the shiny black surface. Judy cursed a blue streak behind them. "Step on it, Mrs. Mac!" The long-awaited news had thrilled then terrified Judy. She knew from her pre-med classes that the human body held roughly five liters of blood. If Kelly lost two liters, she could die.

At the hospital, nurses helped Kelly onto a gurney and rushed her to the maternity ward, taping electrodes to her belly. They shifted Kelly from the gurney to a birthing bed and connected her to monitors. Alarms blared that Colin was in fetal distress. Nurses and doctors buzzed around her, commotion between the stirrups. Every few minutes, a nurse would carry away a saturated towel. Kelly couldn't see over the sphere of her belly, so she finally asked a nurse what was going on.

"Well, what's the worst thing that you thought would happen?"

"That I might need a C-section," Kelly said.

The nurse paused. "Yes. Yes, you will need a C-section."

Through her shock, Kelly understood that was only the tip of the iceberg. They wheeled her from the room, and she saw a bright red heap of used towels on the white tile floor of the bathroom. A nurse shaved her for surgery as they hurried down the hall.

As the gurney pushed through the doors to the operating room, the OR nurse stopped Kelly's sister, her mom, and Judy. "I'm sorry, but you can't come in here."

"Kelly wanted us to stay with her." Her mom said.

The nurse blinked, looked to the surgeon who was donning his blue paper mask, then said, "You need to wait here."

Kelly's sister whitened. Her mother pleaded with the surgeon as he backed through the swinging doors, his hands open before his chest as if holding an invisible crystal ball. The nurse rolled the gurney through, and the anesthesiologist cupped Kelly's nose and mouth with a soft plastic mask. He asked her to count backward from ten.

Kelly whispered, "Ten, nine, eight, seven . . ."

● ● ●

Kelly woke up with something warm and heavy on top of her. It was a thick, heated blanket, and her teeth were chattering. Her sister, Lee, was sitting next to her, watching the hospital room's grainy television. Kelly focused on the silhouettes whipping and spinning before realizing what she was seeing. Figure skating. The Winter Olympics.

Lee noticed Kelly's open eyes. "Colin's doing great," Lee said. "He's beautiful."

The obstetrics nurse opened the door. "How are you feeling?"

"Can I see him?" Kelly asked.

"Soon." The nurse checked Kelly's blood pressure. "Your color's better. We had to give you a couple of blood transfusions."

"What happened?" Kelly asked.

"Placental abruption. Basically, the placenta left your body before the baby did. That's not good, but the surgeons—please, don't try to sit up; you could tear the stitches—the surgeons took care of it. I'll wheel you over to neonatal in a few minutes."

Within the hour, Lee and the nurses arranged Colin on Kelly's chest. Red hair flamed on his round head. *Oh my God*, Kelly thought. *Is that him?* He was twenty-two and a half inches long and weighed eight pounds, four ounces. She had carried him inside her body for nine months, sung to him, taken Lamaze and natural childbirth classes, but she had missed the actual experience of giving birth. One minute she was pregnant; the next minute she had a zipper of stitches running up her empty belly. And then Colin raised his eyes and fixed her with his deep blue gaze. "He's perfect," she said.

ONE O'CLOCK: **Cynthia's Debut**

Cynthia drove her mom's old Chrysler Cirrus, playing a techno CD turned way up and with Emma riding shotgun. They wore matching Victoria's Secret corsets—Cynthia in black and Emma in pink—above skirts and high heels. They hit the clubs in Danbury a lot, sometimes going over to Westchester or down to Manhattan. Cynthia's fake ID said she was eighteen; Emma's said twenty-one, so she could buy drinks. Cynthia only wanted to dance. In the photo, her Goth black hair and dark irises made her face look like a Japanese cartoon, but now she wore her naturally caramel-colored hair in curls. Cynthia stood just over five feet tall, a little bigger than elfin Emma with her ponytail of straight brown hair.

Tiesto, Kaskade, and Scooter shook the speakers while Cynthia and Emma sucked orange juice from sports bottles. They had each dropped a tab of Ecstasy before getting in the car, timing it to kick in when they reached the club. Emma's boyfriend rode with some other guys in the BMW just ahead of them, its tail lights blazing the way down the dark back roads toward the state line.

Emma and Cynthia had known each other for four years, ever since they joined the USASA Cosmos travel soccer team together in seventh grade. Cynthia had started playing soccer in elementary school, but Ethan was like no coach she'd ever had. He was South African, hence the SA in the team's name, and he was serious. He drilled them in footwork, shooting, corner kicks, penalty kicks, and he ran them like crazy. Cynthia could sprint through four quarters, often playing the entire game. When they ran laps, little Emma always straggled at the back of the pack, but Cynthia ran beside her. Ethan hated that. "Shrimp!" That's what he called Cynthia. "You should be at the front!" His voice boomed across the field.

During their third year playing for Ethan, the team went to Florida to compete in a showcase. They had only eleven players, but they made it to the semifinals without substitutes. Then Emma got heat-stroke, so the team carried on with just ten players. Although outnumbered, they managed a tie score at the final whistle. During the penalty kick phase, Ethan had Cynthia take a shot. She planted her foot at the wrong angle and missed the goal. They pulled out the win, but Ethan was still livid with his star player. He pointed out her error, but she already knew what she'd done. They advanced to the finals, and that game also ended with a tie score. Another shootout. Ethan gave Cynthia a second chance, but she did exactly the same thing. Their team lost the trophy.

"What is the matter with you? You know how to do this. You're the best player on this team! You did this in the last game, and we talked about it. How could you make the same mistake again? You lost this game for us! You're off the team!" Ethan stormed around the bench, stuffing equipment into his coaching bag. Cynthia hung her head, but she didn't fold up. She collected water bottles and helped break down the field. As she carried the corner flags to the sideline bench, Ethan approached her. "You've got some sand, Shrimp. Instead of feeling sorry for yourself, you're . . . a better loser than I am. We need you on the team. We'll win next year." That's how he was. He spoke the truth of the moment.

But he didn't bring them to Florida the following year. Ethan died of a sudden heart attack that winter. He had also coached the New Fairfield Prep boys' soccer team, and most of them played on his boys' USASA Cosmos travel team during the off-season. They all wore their team jerseys to the funeral services, as did the girls' team, except for Cynthia, who hadn't heard about the dress code. She wore a black skirt and hoodie, her mascara ruined by tears. A bouquet of purple and white flowers in the pattern of a soccer ball dominated a table beside the coffin, flanked by framed photos of Ethan. His widow, Trish, sat vigil in a bulging black maternity dress, eight months pregnant with their first child.

The two Cosmos teams became much tighter after Ethan's death. They had been planning to go to the World Cup in South Africa together that summer, but instead they watched it on TV. Cynthia convinced her parents to let her quit her private day school so that she could attend the local public high school with her teammates. She and Emma spent a lot more time together during junior year. Every Monday night after the high school football game, a bunch of kids played barefoot soccer until the stadium lights went out and then went looking for a party. Tonight they were heading to a new place called Heaven and Hell.

They pulled into the club's parking lot and got out of the car. The neon lights were just starting to sizzle, and Cynthia and Emma both floated from their car in the blissful state that gives Ecstasy its name. Emma's boyfriend wrapped an arm around her, and his friend sidled up next to Cynthia. His breath smelled sweetly of rum; they'd been drinking Caribou Lous in the BMW. The four walked past a grill cook serving burgers on the patio and stepped through the front doors into flashing lights. Scooter's "Crank It Up" rattled the glass. The air smelled metallic and perfumed. In the darkness, Cynthia could see horned heads and halos, pitchforks and wings. It took her a moment to realize that this wasn't a typical nightclub.

"Emma, it's a rave!"

The devil-girls wore leather S&M outfits, thigh-high boots, and Cleopatra eyeliner. The angels wore lacy bras that pushed up glittering cleavage. The guys wore dress shirts, mostly unbuttoned. One man was shirtless, red makeup covering his face and body, black moustache and goatee spiking off his face. He drank from a long horn that he rested against his potbelly. The crowd danced hard in a grind of electronic music and a patchwork of colored lights.

"We're the only ones without costumes!" Cynthia shouted into Emma's ear.

"I know! I feel so stupid!"

They wove through the crowd toward a corner of the room. Colored lasers sliced through the acrid vapor of the fog machine. When they reached a spiral staircase, Cynthia gripped the railings and scampered up.

The upper level had a different feel. The music leaned more toward trance, less industrial. The angels here danced with more sensuality. In the crowded shadows, Cynthia occasionally glimpsed Emma's face—now bleached white, now dark, now soaked in a flash of rabid color. The music was fluid and upbeat. Everyone moved in sync, like a school of fish flowing as a collective wave, rippling with liquid light. The boys left early, but Cynthia and Emma danced for hours, only pausing to refill their water bottles and top off with another tab of E. They all met up later at Emma's boyfriend's apartment. After Heaven and Hell, the rest of the night was nearer to Eden. Cynthia had never felt so good.

ONE O'CLOCK: **Call to Adventure**

Every tale has a beginning. After setting the stage, every story gets moving when something upsets the status quo. Perhaps a bargain or challenge is struck, as when Jack exchanges his cow for magic beans. Cinderella's story begins when she learns of the palace ball from a royal courier. Zeus sends his messenger, Hermes, to launch Odysseus's epic voyage home, but Luke Skywalker starts his journey in the opposite direction when he hears Princess Leia's hologram begging for Obi-Wan Kenobi's help. In these examples, the heroes heed their respective Calls to Adventure, diverging from their ordinary routines and setting their journeys in motion.

Colin's story began before he was even born. Kelly's predicament put her at a crossroads with no easy path to choose. Abortion? Adoption? Awkward paternity tests followed by gold-digger accusations? Choosing single motherhood was the first step in Kelly's parenting adventure, and the first hour of Colin's decades-long quest.

Forty percent[2] of American babies are born to unmarried moms like Kelly. The nuclear family remains our idealized concept of the social norm, but many kids today grow up in divided or blended families. Ironically, lots of ancient and modern heroes also rose from unorthodox family situations.

Athena, Apollo, Artemis, Hermes, Persephone, Dionysus, Perseus, Hercules, Helen of Troy, Minos, and all nine Muses resulted from Zeus's philandering. If that sounds scandalous, consider some even more shocking origin stories: The Hindu god Vishnu impregnated Devaki and was thus himself reborn as Krishna. The virginal Egyptian goddess Isis miraculously conceived the sky god Horus. The Aztec goddess Coatlicue collected a bundle of feathers against her bosom, which impregnated her with the sun god Huitzilopochtli. In *The Hero with a Thousand Faces*, Joseph Campbell dedicates almost twenty pages to virgin births. Perhaps those ancient myths were conceived as allegories for the quotidian reality, as common then as now: fatherless children. In your favorite book or movie, is the protagonist part of a traditional nuclear family? Or is his or her family tree more complicated? How about your own family structure?

Other heroes have less-supernatural childhoods. In Sir Thomas Malory's fifteenth-century story collection *Le Morte d'Arthur*, King Arthur grows up in an adoptive family, unaware that his real father was Uther Pendragon until he pulls the famous sword from the stone. In a later chapter, Sir Lancelot abandons his lover and their unborn son. When the boy turns fifteen, he joins the Round Table as Sir Galahad and reunites with his father. In contemporary echoes of these medieval tales, Luke Skywalker is secretly raised by surrogate parents. When he inherits his father's light saber, he sets off to become a Jedi knight. Harry Potter lives with his aunt and uncle on Privet Drive, ignorant of his parents' true identities until magical letters arrive on his eleventh birthday. His cruel, adoptive family whisks him away to a remote, seaside cottage, but the letters pursue them, ultimately followed by Hagrid on his flying motorcycle. Harry's Call to Adventure ruptures the Status Quo. He will no longer live in the cupboard under the stairs but in a boarding school for young wizards. In all of these cases, as in Colin's, the blood flowing through the hero's veins foreshadows his inevitable quest of self-discovery.

The Call to Adventure is not always genetically predestined. In a courageous twist, Katniss Everdeen volunteers to accept *another's* fate. Her normal life of hardscrabble survival in an oppressed mining town is disrupted when her younger sister's name is drawn from the lottery, earning her a place among the child gladiators in that year's Hunger Games. Katniss steps forward to spare her defenseless sister, the first hour of her hero's journey.

Joseph Campbell notes a dramatic device that often follows the Call to Adventure that he terms "the Refusal of the Call." Odysseus and Achilles initially refuse enlistment in the Trojan War. Arthur is shocked when he draws the sword from the stone, certain that he is unfit to rule. In J. R. R. Tolkien's books, both Bilbo and Frodo initially resist Gandalf's invitation. Even Luke Skywalker declines to help Obi-Wan save Princess Leia, only changing his mind after finding his home burned to the ground. Peter Parker gains supernatural powers from a spider's bite but squanders his gifts. He witnesses a crime in progress but refuses to stop the criminal, who later murders his Uncle Ben. At last Peter vows to fight crime as Spider-Man.

Fictional stories tend to be dramatic, but real-life Calls to Adventure are often less definitive. Cynthia's heroic cycle began very subtly. Her first exposure to the rave party scene opened the door to a thrilling escape from her mundane suburban life. It seemed like such a small thing, an incremental escalation in her active nightlife. How could she have known that siren's call was her first slip down a cascade into bigger risks, harder drugs, deeper trouble, and increasing self-destruction? Cynthia seems as curious and innocent as Alice, who followed a strange rabbit only to tumble into her bizarre *Adventures in Wonderland*. Alice's journey offers an allegory for adventures like Cynthia's—a confused and headlong exploration of an alien world both enchanting and dangerous.

The allegorical power of Alice's tale continues to resonate in today's stories, 150 years later. Neo, the reluctant hero of *The Matrix*, awakens to a mysterious Call to Adventure on his computer that directs him to "follow the white rabbit." A moment later, a group of Goth punks appear at his door, inviting Neo to leave the safety of his home for an underground nightclub. At first he declines their invitation, then he spots a rabbit tattoo on one of their arms. He decides to follow, and his journey begins.

In real life, the Call to Adventure can be positive or negative, public or secret, obvious or subtle. It can be as overt as a sports team tryout, a job offer, or a college acceptance letter. It can also be as cryptic as an unnamed yearning, only recognized in hindsight as the first step. We meet dozens of people every day, and most of them cross the stage of our lives with little effect. Only later do we discover who will return to play more than a passing role.

As teenagers move through their academic, athletic, and social schedules, they encounter all sorts of temptations, invitations, and fascinations. Some they will refuse. Others they will accept—perhaps immediately, perhaps eventually. Whether they realize it or not, every such moment is a fork in the road. Each decision could be insignificant, or it could be the first step on a new, heroic journey.

Consider the young people you mentor. What Calls to Adventure are they hearing? Which Calls have they refused? Which have they answered?

Now ask the same questions of yourself. How do you know when a new story begins in real life? Sometimes it's obvious: moving to a new hometown, the first day at a new school or new job. Other beginnings are only clear in retrospect. Lots of first dates don't lead to marriage, but every marriage starts with a first date. Looking back, can you identify the Calls to Adventure in your own past? How did they disrupt the equilibrium of your life? Which Calls did you refuse? Which did you accept? Why?

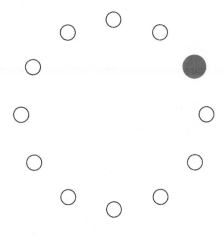

CHAPTER 2

Assistance

In a typical quest story, after the hero has accepted the Call to Adventure, he or she receives some form of assistance—a companion, a powerful artifact, or a secret word. When Perseus sets off to kill Medusa, Athena and Hermes give him winged sandals, a shield, and a sickle. The MI6 quartermaster gives James Bond new gadgets whenever he leaves on a mission. Such a moment marks two o'clock on the hero's journey.

TWO O'CLOCK: **Colin's Support System**

Kelly opened boxes of digital switches in the narrow shipping office beside the loading dock at Rochester Telephone. She fixated on the box cutter in her hand, a triangle of shining steel slipped from the handle. It cut through cardboard so effortlessly. It could easily slice open her body. In the silence of that cell-like room, surrounded by blank-faced boxes bathed in fluorescent light, Kelly caressed the flesh of her arm with that thin razor. Lulled by the barely audible hum of electrical current, she slipped into a kind of trance, the point of the metal blade tracing a cold line up and down the inside of her forearm.

She had cardboard boxes at home to unpack too. She and Colin had just moved out of their first home, a charming old colonial with chunky molding and warped glass in the window panes. The wind blew right through the drafty house. They kept the heat down in winter and wore thick sweaters. They shared the three-bedroom house with Mandy, who worked as a waitress while taking classes at the local community college. Because of her dinner-shift work schedule, they rarely crossed paths.

That had been their home for three years, allowing Kelly to work her way up the ranks of Highland Telephone and scrape together some savings. She planned to spend it on Sunshine Day Care, a top-notch program run by two certified teachers. Sunshine only accepted six children each fall, and they liked Colin's intelligence, imagination, and sense of humor. It was expensive, but Kelly was in line for a promotion to management. Colin had already been through a series of off-the-books babysitters, but they were all the same: eight hours of supervised television. She couldn't wait to enroll him at Sunshine.

Then Rochester Telephone bought Highland. The new company's policies required all managers to have at least a two-year Associate of Arts degree. No degree, no promotion. Kelly tried to stay positive and devise a new strategy, but her old VW Rabbit stalled for the last time, and she spent all her savings to replace it. Then Mandy moved out. Kelly paid both halves of the rent while she searched for a new housemate, but her savings ran out before she found one, so she and Colin found a tiny bungalow in another town. When Sunshine Day Care called to confirm Colin's enrollment, Kelly had to decline.

Three years after moving out of her parents' house, their family of two was still barely treading water: a dead-end job, a subcompact home, TV day care, and another sputtering old car. Kelly felt like she was failing Colin and that he would be better off without her. Her profound sorrow had faded into a kind of detached apathy, a poison gas that filled her nerveless body as she stroked the thin membrane of her skin with that thin razor blade.

Something compelled her to pick up the phone. She felt as though she'd been screaming for months with her hand over her own mouth—until that moment. She called Lisa, her friend from church. "I'm in the back room at work, unpacking circuit boxes, and I'm running the box cutter up and down my arm. I'm wondering that if I cut myself, will I'll bleed."

The way that Kelly spoke made Lisa's hair stand on end. "I'll be right there." Within forty-eight hours, Kelly was admitted to Westchester Mental Health Center while four-year-old Colin stayed with his grandparents. Colin's aunt and uncle, Vicki and Jim, came over with their boys, Ryan and Reece, aged five and three years old. Colin knew them from holiday gatherings and big family events, but they didn't see one another more than a few times a year. The boys played together while the four adults talked things over. Kelly had been diagnosed with major depression. She would be in the hospital for at least two months.

After the discussion, Jim pulled Colin aside. "Colin, your mom's sick, and she's going to be okay, but she needs to stay in the hospital for a while. We think it would be best—and the most fun for you— to come live with us and be with the boys and do things over at our house until she gets better."

"Okay," Colin said. "Can I go play now?"

• • •

For nine months, Colin lived with his Aunt Vicki and Uncle Jim and went to preschool with his cousins. The lifestyle was everything Kelly had wanted for Colin but couldn't provide. He got to take care of the dog, goats, and other animals at the preschool. In the afternoons, Uncle Jim took the boys hiking in the state forest behind their rural home. They followed the colored blazes in autumn, winter, and spring, staying on the marked trails and learning all the animal tracks.

The boys were best friends and closest rivals, more like siblings than cousins. They shared a room with a triple bunk bed. They stacked wooden block castles up to the ceiling and built forts out of sofa cushions and blankets. If there were three different-colored cups, they all wanted the blue one. During the weekly ritual of making ice-cream sundaes, they always tried to outdo one another; Colin's trademark tactic was to reach for an outrageous flourish—an olive, or something from the spice cabinet. He may have been the only five-year-old to eat cumin and black pepper ice cream.

Bath time was a big part of each day. The solid old house had a huge claw-foot tub that could hold all three boys at once. One evening, as Colin zoomed around the bathroom, his feet got tangled in a towel, tripping him face-first into the toilet. He popped up gasping, his trademark machine-gun laugh ripping through the house. Vicki tossed him back into the soap suds while his cousins joined the cackling.

The house had a steep staircase, which the boys turned into a contest. They took turns jumping from higher and higher steps. Little Reece gave up at the seventh, but Ryan and Colin pushed each other to the next level, springing into the air from the ninth step and landing on rubber legs at the bottom. That tenth step was a taunting Everest to both Ryan and Colin. Who would be first to conquer it? Jim knew the game would end with cracked floorboards or broken bones, or both, so he gave them cushions from the camper, which they used for sledding down the staircase instead.

Colin's sojourn was not all smooth sailing. Kelly had treated Colin as a partner in their two-person family, although he was only in preschool. She'd nurtured his impulses but held him accountable to responsibilities beyond his age. The rules were different at Aunt Vicki's house: less self-reliance and less autonomy. One Sunday Colin insisted on wearing sneakers to church, but Jim laid down the law. They were standing at the door of the boys' bedroom.

"You need to change your shoes, Colin."

"No, these are fine."

"Actually, you have to wear the loafers."

Colin tried to squeeze past him to the stairs.

Jim gripped Colin's arm. "Colin, I'm done arguing about this. You're going to take off your sneakers and put on your shoes, or I'm going to do it for you. Period."

Colin's fury flared behind his eyes; Jim saw it there, white-hot like his own, like his father's—the Mac temper. Colin kicked off his sneakers and stamped into the loafers, storming down the stairs to the car. Jim watched with unease at the size of the fire trapped in such a little kid.

When Halloween approached, Jim attached spare hoses and tubes to boxy backpacks and added tiny lightbulbs from Radio Shack. Vicki bought three white coveralls and sewed patches on them. The three cousins had the best Ghostbusters costumes in the neighborhood. Kids in plain store-bought costumes envied their flickering Christmas lights. Colin wished his mom could have seen it, but Kelly was still in the hospital.

She slowly put herself back together with counseling and medication, but her delicate state permitted few visits. The first time Colin went to see Kelly, he transformed when he stepped inside the massive converted mansion. His energetic personality folded in upon itself like origami. He looked straight ahead as they walked through the big, heavy doors and down the oversized hallways. When he saw his mom, he flew to her. She enveloped him in a huge, soft hug, and he seemed to shrink into her.

"Hi, buddy. How are you?"

Colin shrugged.

"I missed you. Did you miss me?"

Colin nodded.

"How was Halloween?"

Colin shrugged.

Kelly was released in time for Christmas, but with certain conditions. She moved back home to their bungalow, alone. She quit her job at the phone company and signed up for classes at the community college, supported by her parents. Every night she joined Jim's family for dinner and put Colin to bed before returning home, alone. In June, after a full semester like this, Kelly's doctors decided that she was ready to resume full-time parenting. Colin graduated from preschool in June and moved back home.

Kelly drove from her brother's house with Colin in the back, along with his few bags of clothes and toys. He unbuckled himself and opened the car door, racing past her down the stone steps to the front door of their squat blue bungalow in its patch of grass. *He moves so fast*, Kelly thought. Her hand trembled a little as she fit the key in the lock, and she felt her breathing quicken. Colin burst past her and inside, bouncing off the walls as she unpacked his bags in his own room. *So much energy*. She remembered the admonition of her psychologist: "You think he's challenging you, but he's not. He just needs to make sure you're strong enough. That you're able to take care of him." She paralyzed Colin with tickles, his woodpecker laugh filling their tiny home.

TWO O'CLOCK: Cynthia Meets Paul

Cynthia graduated with a soccer scholarship to Pace University, and she worked at CVS for the summer. She wore a photo-booth lab coat over her light-blue polo shirt and a khaki skirt from her private school days. Her boss was super-strict. If she told you to "face the shelves," she expected you to tidy the whole store and then come back when you were done and ask her what else you could do. No talking. No detours. Work was a breeze when her boss wasn't there. Cynthia read magazines and took extra-long "ten-minute" breaks when Paul stopped by, then went to raves and parties with Emma at night. Overall, the summer was shaping up perfectly.

One day Paul drove over with his new kitten. It was a Maine coon cat with orange hair, so tiny that it still had a potbelly with peach fuzz. They sat in Paul's car in the CVS parking lot while it cried and wobbled all over Cynthia's lap. She held it against her collar and let it lick her neck.

"He likes you," Paul said. He was tall, thin, and he usually wore a polo shirt and basketball shorts, his baseball cap cocked to the side. He had brown hair and kind eyes in a baby face. He was a year behind Cynthia in school, and they'd never really hung out, but she had bought pot from him once.

"He's a cutie. Oh, I wish I could take him home."

"He keeps scratching the couch."

"Bad kitty."

"I'd better go home before he takes a piss in my mom's car." He lived right around the corner from CVS and visited her when he wasn't working at the Feed Barn on Route 7.

"Yeah, I've been on my ten-minute break for like an hour."

"Hey, what are you doing on Saturday?"

"I have to work until nine-thirty."

"After that, you want to go bowling?"

"Bowling?"

"Yeah."

"Okay."

● ● ●

When Paul picked Cynthia up at CVS, she had already changed. She wore high heels but had socks in her purse for the bowling shoes. She climbed into his Honda Civic, the summer twilight soaked in humidity.

"You want some of this?" Paul showed her two pills with a capital G impressed into one side and a trucker's mud-flap silhouette of a naked woman on the other. Cynthia knew this brand of Ecstasy: Gs up, hoes down, like the Snoop Dogg song.

"Sure." He tipped the tablets into Cynthia's hand, and she chased them with his orange juice.

Paul drove down Route 7 to the bowling alley as they listened to techno songs. In the settling darkness, car headlights beamed and signs on the Miracle Mile glowed more vibrantly and more cheerfully than usual. When they pulled into the Brookfield Lanes parking lot, the square halogen floodlights posted at the perimeter shone like welcoming beacons in space. In the creamy light under the porch roof, Paul held the glass door open for Cynthia. They stepped out of the humid night and into the chilled and dazzling world of "Cosmic Bowling."

Cynthia smelled the snack bar's salty popcorn, tough pizza, and industrial onion rings. Disco balls spewed white diamonds on every surface. Colored lasers sliced designs on the walls and ceiling, out of sync with the classic rock videos blaring from the far wall. Above each lane, rectangular screens blazed fiery red with score grids or cold blue with an ad for Dollar-Night Sunday. That train of twenty-four televisions stretched across the dark ceiling from left to right like stepping-stones of bright glass. Beneath the rock music, the clatter of pins rang almost constantly, each set tumbling down only to rise again.

Cynthia watched her feet connect with the black-lit carpet, a repeating pattern of white stars and rocket ships, green and red planets popping out of a deep blue-violet background. People who passed her had glowing eyeballs, phosphorescent T-shirts, and purple teeth. Seeing the arcade games, she remembered Gina Epalito's twelfth birthday party, when Jeanette Silver had tripped with her bowling ball and gotten a bloody nose. The memory made her laugh, even though it wasn't funny at the time.

She and Paul rented shoes and a lane, then went to the bar. Paul saw one of his older brother's friends and asked him to buy two screwdrivers. He took the plastic cups with a wink and led Cynthia over to lane eight. Paul entered their names into the Day-Glo buttons of the scoring console, mesmerizing under the black light. They bowled four games, cheering whether they hit the pins or not.

"You two need to settle down," a lady in the next lane said.

Cynthia covered her mouth and giggled.

"Cosmic Bowling!" Paul told the lady. "Cosmic Bowling!" he cheered at Cynthia.

After the game, they took another dose in the parking lot and drove around looking at the kaleidoscope of cars' lights and traffic signals. They ended up in the parking lot behind the massive brick school district offices. They tangled around each other in the parked car, sparkling with the electricity of a first kiss. Paul wanted to go all the way, but Cynthia wouldn't. Not on the first date.

They spread a blanket in the parking lot to look at the stars. Lying on their backs and staring at the Milky Way, they held hands and laughed at the fussy lady at the bowling alley. Cynthia talked about the Pace soccer team, about her dream of becoming a lawyer. When a shooting star drifted across the sky in a lazy spectacle of searing light, Cynthia made a wish.

TWO O'CLOCK: **Assistance**

After accepting the Call to Adventure, the hero receives some form of Assistance before setting off on his or her journey. Depending on the circumstances, it might be a sword or a laser gun, a magic spell or just good advice. It might even be a helpful companion, who joins the hero on the journey. Indeed, the English word "mentor" comes from such a character in Homer's *Odyssey*. While Odysseus was fighting the Trojan War, Mentor handled the care and education of the king's son, Telemachus. This boy grew up and left home on his own quest.

Modern stories contain obvious examples of this stage of the monomyth. Q gives James Bond new gadgets at the beginning of every mission. Before leaving his home planet, Luke Skywalker gains his father's light saber and the friendship of Obi-Wan Kenobi, Han Solo, Chewbacca, R2-D2, and C-3PO. Merlin appears to guide Arthur after he draws the sword from the stone. Haymitch trains Katniss Everdeen to survive the Hunger Games. Harry Potter comes of age, and Hagrid arrives to transport him to Hogwarts. All heroes rely on some sort of Assistance during their journey; even heroes need help.

Adults are not the only mentors in a hero's life. Harry Potter learns as much from Ron and Hermione as he does from his teachers at Hogwarts. Bilbo and Frodo heed Gandalf's advice but also take lessons from their other comrades. Sometimes, Assistance is tangled up in romance. Peeta Mellark is Katniss Everdeen's partner in the Hunger Games, helping her win the deadly contest while teaching her about trust. Whether sage counselor or equal partner, fancy weapon or potent words, the Assistance gained at two o'clock empowers the hero throughout his or her journey.

Colin's school year with his grandparents, aunt, uncle, and cousins filled him with a bulletproof sense of security that he would take for granted throughout his life: Your family will always be there to catch you. It would never occur to Colin that he might find himself helpless and alone in the future. Without ever articulating the concept in so many words, he knew that the McIntyre clan was an unbreakable safety net. This article of faith sustains him throughout his journey, as we shall see.

Cynthia's story begins at a later stage in her life. Young children look to their parents as role models, but adolescents push away. That rejection is a healthy and necessary step toward establishing an independent identity, but it leaves a void to be filled. Cynthia's soccer coach served as a positive role model, like the noble Jedi master Obi-Wan Kenobi. When Coach Ethan died, his absence left a void that remained unfilled until Paul exposed Cynthia to a whole new dimension of risk and excitement, the path to the Dark Side. And she didn't even see it coming.

Consider your own past. Who were your friends while growing up? Who pushed the boundaries alongside you? What did you learn from them? Now consider your mentors from the older generation. That list probably starts with your parents, but what other adult influenced you during your school years? Who taught you the lessons that stick with you today? This lens flips both ways. You were once the pupil, but now you are the mentor. If your students answer this question years from now, your name might arise. How will they describe the Assistance they received from you?

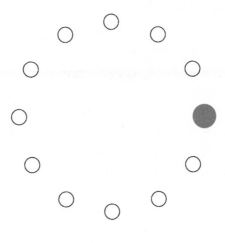

CHAPTER 3

Departure

The hero's ordinary world has an outer limit, a boundary that is dangerous to cross. If you are a Knight of the Round Table, you ride from Camelot in search of adventure. If you are a hobbit, you leave the Shire. The hero departs from his ordinary world at three o'clock.

THREE O'CLOCK: **Colin Notices**

Kelly lay in Colin's bed and sang to him, as she did every night after reading books to him. They had lived in the bungalow for almost a year now, and Colin was winding down his first year of kindergarten. She pushed the red hair off his forehead and sang the nightly finale of their bedtime routine, John Denver's "Tools." Kelly kissed him goodnight, turned out the light, and settled on the living room couch with her college textbook. This habit was firmly established, a predictable daily regimen that fortified Colin's sense of security and demonstrated Kelly's authority.

A moment later, Colin stood in front of her. "Read me another book," he said.

"Colin, get into bed. Reading time is over. You know the deal."

He didn't budge.

"Colin, get into bed."

"Read me another book."

"Colin, no. Get into bed."

He stormed off. Kelly raised her eyebrows and reopened her textbook, but Colin reappeared holding a baseball bat.

"Read. Me. Another. Book."

Kelly studied Colin. His blue eyes seethed in his reddening face, his mouth thin as a wire. *What is up with him?* She thought. "Colin, I love you, but this behavior is unacceptable. I already said good night to you. It's time for you to go to sleep. Getting out of bed and threatening me is totally out of line, and you know that."

Colin just stood and glared at her, an ember of fury behind each eye.

Kelly glared back.

After a long few minutes, Kelly said softly, "Bedtime."

Colin stomped back to bed.

What is happening to him!? Kelly pulled the parenting guides down from her bookshelf and stayed up half the night rereading them.

• • •

A few days later, at an end-of-year meeting with Colin's kindergarten teacher, Kelly sat in an adult-size chair in the Lilliputian classroom. Construction paper collages decorated the walls.

Ms. Fabrise sat across from her, wearing a print blouse and colorful, chunky earrings. After acknowledging Colin's intelligence, she wanted to talk about his stubborn streak. "Earlier this week the class made cards for Father's Day, but Colin refused to participate. He told me, 'I don't have a father.' Can you believe that? I told him that I would be speaking with you about it." Ms. Fabrise wore a smug expression.

Kelly held her breath for a long moment. She envisioned this room full of chattering kids, a buzzing hive of safety scissors, glue, and markers. She imagined Colin surrounded by his peers making trophies for their dads. What an outcast. He must have felt belittled and betrayed, exiled in his own skin.

At last Kelly said, "As a matter of fact, Colin doesn't have a father. He was telling you the truth."

Ms. Fabrise froze and then fumbled an apology, but Kelly knew it was too late. The genie was out of the bottle, and their lives would never be the same.

THREE O'CLOCK: **Cynthia Crosses the Line**

Cynthia straightened papers behind the register and watched Dale working behind the prescription counter at the other side of the store. It was July, and she'd been at New Milford Pharmacy since February. Things were still great with Paul, but they hadn't gone so well at Pace University. She'd become inexplicably ill during the fall soccer season, unable to keep any food down, just like another time in tenth grade. Sipping Sprite through a straw, she tried to make it to midterms, but the doctors sent her home and prescribed an intravenous potassium drip three times a week. Cynthia got better quickly and wanted to return to school, but Pace made her wait until the new term in January. She began her spring semester with a new roommate, zero credits, and a rerun of all her fall courses.

At the same time, CVS started requiring more work hours of part-timers, but Cynthia's class schedule was too tight. Luckily she found a weekend job at the only other pharmacy in town, on the corner of Bank and Main near the village green post office. They sold greeting cards, photo frames, and children's toys along with medicine and beauty supplies. Historic photos of downtown hung on the dingy walls of the old store, and the dropped ceiling always felt a little too low, but at least she could earn some money when she came home on the weekends to visit Paul.

Cynthia started the spring term with good grades, but she fell sick in April with the same symptoms. Her illness once again confounded all the doctors. They thought it might be abdominal migraines, a poorly understood affliction. Cynthia recovered after returning home, just like before. Due to her extensive absences, Pace asked her not to return in the fall. She had no college credits, no soccer scholarship, and no plan for next year.

Paul was the only silver lining. They'd spent almost every weekend together, including his senior prom. While all their friends sat on couches outside the hotel ballroom, stoned as rocks, she and Paul stayed sober and danced to every song. Cynthia wore a full-length evening gown that matched Paul's blue satin vest and tie. She'd lost so much weight from her illness that a seamstress had to alter her dress at the last minute.

Since the prom, she'd more or less been living at Paul's house. His parents insisted that she sleep on an air mattress in Paul's room, but he always ended up beside her anyway. Sometimes, as she dozed off, she could hear Paul's brother, Andy, crushing tablets with his mortar and pestle in the next bedroom. He was a major drug fiend and dealer. Paul only dealt a little, but he'd tried almost every drug and was always sampling new ones.

Paul's curious attitude prompted Cynthia to notice the tiny cardboard cubes on the prescription counter at work. They reminded her of the little Milk Duds boxes she used to get on Halloween, except these were pills labeled "not for resale." On impulse, she grabbed a bunch and stuffed them in her purse. After work she showed Paul and asked if he wanted to try them. He inspected one box but didn't open it. "You might be able to get a few bucks for these. Let me call some people."

He dialed a number and read the chemical name into the phone. "Three boxes, two tabs of 500 milligrams each," he said. "Yeah, sure. OK. Peace." He turned to Cynthia. "Can you get more?"

"Yeah, I think so."

"Are there any cameras in there?"

"No." Cynthia said.

"You're sure?"

"Yeah. They joke about how there's no security at all."

Paul's cheeks were so smooth. She would do anything he asked.

"We can get fifty bucks a pill. This is three hundred dollars right here. How many can you get?"

"I don't know."

• • •

Now Cynthia kept her eye on the pharmacy in the back of the store, waiting for Dale to go into the back office so that she could snag more of the little boxes. She and Paul might use the money to splurge on a Manhattan hotel or buy a used car. Dale puttered behind the high counter, lining up the medications he'd prepared. Cynthia stepped around her register and pretended to organize the candy bars.

"Cynthia, can you keep an eye on things for a minute? I'll be right back," Dale said.

"Sure." Cynthia knew he played online poker in the office. "No problem."

When he closed the door to the back room, she silently opened the gate to the prescriptions counter and ducked through it. Her hearing seemed to dim. She looked through the front windows, but nobody was coming. She scanned the pharmacy desk for the samples. The countertop was full of white bags, each one sealed by a colorful label bearing that customer's name. Except one.

She opened the bag, and it crinkled loudly in the empty store. There were just as many samples as yesterday. She considered taking the whole bag, but what if Dale noticed? She took eight more boxes, stuffed four in each pocket, and slipped out to the racks of Band-Aids, deodorant, and shampoo. She faced the shelves, pulling the bottles and cans forward, lining them up in neat rows.

Eleven hundred dollars in two days. Eleven hundred dollars! And the drug company reps were dropping off samples all the time.

THREE O'CLOCK: **Departure**

At this point in the story, the hero leaves his or her ordinary world and enters a new one. In Homer's *Odyssey*, Odysseus begins his quest to return home by sailing off on his makeshift raft. After surviving

Poseidon's wrath, he reaches the shores of an unfamiliar land. Naked and exhausted, he collapses into a bed of leaves. Meanwhile, his son, Telemachus, receives advice from the goddess Athena (disguised as Odysseus's friend Mentor). Telemachus orders the suitors wooing his grieving mother to leave their property. "I hold the reins of power in this house," he declares to his mother, signaling his departure from boyhood. With that statement, he crosses the threshold into adulthood, mirrored by his physical departure for Pylos and Sparta on a dangerous quest for news of his missing father.

Like Telemachus, Colin lacks a father figure in his life. Colin's journey begins with the sudden, simplistic epiphany that his nuclear family is missing a key piece. His naive self-esteem cracks against the hidden edge of a benign holiday, permanently fracturing his perception of himself. As he ages, this fault line expands, slowly ripping against his confidence. Colin's heroic struggle is a fight to seal that invisible interior wound.

At three o'clock in the cycle, Colin sees himself with new perspective, a bit like Harry Potter when he discovers the secret truth on his eleventh birthday. After Hagrid finds Harry in the Dursleys' seaside hideout, Hagrid chastises Harry's uncle: "You never told him? Never told him what was in the letter Dumbledore left fer him? I was there! I saw Dumbledore leave it, Dursley! An' you've kept it from him all these years?" With this revelation, Harry leaves his Muggle identity behind as he launches into the wizarding world on Hagrid's flying motorcycle. Likewise, the boy Arthur unintentionally stumbles upon his destiny to rule Britain when he draws the sword from the stone. He doesn't travel across a geographic boundary, but he enters a new world of self-awareness, political intrigue, and the burden of responsibility.

Cynthia's Departure doesn't expose a hidden secret. She impulsively decides to cross an invisible line and then commits to the chain reaction that follows. Think of Alice propelled to the rabbit hole by her curiosity and tumbling into the unknown. Dorothy overreacts when her dog, Toto, is threatened, running away on impulse as a tornado approaches. Katniss Everdeen doesn't plan to enter the Hunger

Games, but a snap decision sends her speeding toward her doom in The Capitol. Cynthia has drifted away from shady escapism and into the deeper shadows of crime. She moves into Paul's house—literally crossing a threshold—and slips from drug user to drug thief and drug dealer. Neither Cynthia nor Colin planned their Departures. Neither did Alice and Arthur.

As the story shifts from one world to the other, the change of scenery outside reflects a change happening inside the hero. Alice must grapple with the bizarre and confounding rules of Wonderland. Dorothy must navigate magical Oz. Harry gains his freedom from the Dursleys but must prove himself at Hogwarts. The story's jarring new setting reflects the hero's inner turmoil.

The contrast between the ordinary and special worlds is usually drastic, and this sudden, dramatic transition makes for a good story. In real life, this evolution is often more incremental and uneven. Teens cling to the safety of their childhood personae, while simultaneously reaching for adult status and privileges. The tension within this split identity fuels years of turmoil until a cohesive, mature personality finally emerges. For adolescents, this process is messy and unpredictable, progressing in stops and starts with plenty of inconsistency. They may be ahead of the curve in some respects, while blooming late in other areas.

Along the way, teens dip into all sorts of mischief, testing the waters of illicit drugs and other taboos. These obvious missteps often "seem like a good idea at the time." This can be explained neurologically. The "incentive processing system" peaking in teenagers' brains makes them more "sensation seeking, more emotionally reactive, and more attentive to social information."[3] Meanwhile, the countervailing "cognitive control system" is still catching up. The maturity to suppress impulses peaks after twenty years of age—too late to protect teens from their rash decisions. So, with their inchoate brains, adolescents decide how to spend their Friday nights, often breaching thresholds better left uncrossed.

Once again, call to mind your favorite book or movie. Is there a moment when the hero leaves behind his or her familiar world and sets off into the unknown? Although the hero's journey truly begins with the Call and Assistance, the moment of Departure usually involves travel. Does your hero cross the tracks into the wrong side of town, or fly through a wormhole into an unknown galaxy? More subtle stories revolve around an interior journey in which the hero departs from a place of emotional equilibrium and must struggle through a field of psychological obstacles. The most engaging monomyth stories involve both interpersonal and intrapersonal plotlines, each reflecting the other.

How does the Departure stage echo in your life? Think of the Calls to Adventure that you listed at the end of the first chapter. Did your Departure take the shape of geographical movement? An emotional shift? Both? What was the unknown territory that you entered? Why was it unfamiliar? The next six stages of the hero's journey take place in that heretofore unexplored special world.

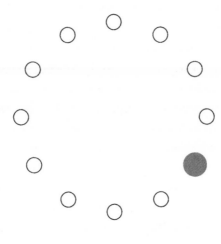

CHAPTER 4

Trials

A fter crossing into the Special World, the hero faces challenges. Soon after leaving Tatooine, Luke Skywalker rescues Princess Leia, gets trapped in a trash compactor, and escapes from the Death Star. While living at Hogwarts, Harry Potter juggles homework, Quidditch practice, and extracurricular detective work. The hero's mettle is tested during this fourth hour of the heroic cycle.

FOUR O'CLOCK: **Colin's Uphill Climb**

Colin rode the bus to Pine Tree Elementary School every weekday and spent Saturdays at his soccer or baseball games. On the surface, he was just like the other second graders, but he couldn't escape the taboo of his origins. Every time Kelly registered Colin for Little League, she had to bring his birth certificate. In the box for "Father" there was no name, just "———," a universal Morse code for "No dad." At the PTA meetings and birthday parties, other parents smiled politely, but Kelly sensed their sanctimony. Colin's teacher offered an intended compliment: "He's very bright. You'd never know he comes from a single-parent home." When Colin got into a shouting match at the bus stop, the other kid's dad knocked on Kelly's door that evening. As Kelly endured his rant, something turned in her stomach. She knew he wouldn't have had the guts to talk that way to the man of the house.

Sundays at the United Methodist Church were their safe haven. Kelly taught Sunday school, and Colin joined the youth group, which staged plays, made arts and crafts, and went on overnight retreats. The minister and congregation embraced them both as valued members of the community. Kelly earned a "spiritual counselor" credential through the church and facilitated the youth group on Sunday mornings. They focused on local service projects and personal plans for the future. One week a boy opened up about his grandfather's death. "Kelly, I don't get it. My grandfather was sick, and we prayed and prayed and prayed for him to get better, and then he died. The minister said that it was a blessing. How is that a blessing? Why didn't God answer our prayers?"

Kelly knew all about frustrated hopes. "That's the hardest question of faith," she said, "but you have to understand that God doesn't send lightning bolts out of the sky to spare us pain. That's not how it works. He's with us *in* our pain." This wisdom helped Kelly make sense of the world, but she knew it was a lot for a teenager to absorb.

Colin's grandpa played a big part in his life too. Kelly's dad lived forty minutes away, but he drove Colin to the barber every month and watched him play every soccer and baseball game. Whenever Colin and Kelly came to visit, Grandpa asked, "Do you want to watch *Star Wars?*" They watched the whole trilogy straight through, Colin eating popcorn from a giant silver mixing bowl, lying on the brown carpet just a few feet from the huge television. When one movie was finished, Colin pressed eject and swapped cassettes in the VCR. If he slept over, Grandpa drove him into town in his restored BMW Bavaria to buy the morning newspapers. He and Colin washed the car together on sunny afternoons.

Kelly witnessed their relationship with a combination of joy, gratitude, and envy. This was not how Mr. Mac had raised his own kids.

He was the head of the department in Pine Bush until he retired after thirty-six years of teaching English, coaching football, and chaperoning school dances. He was the first one at school in the morning, always impeccably dressed in jacket and tie. In his spare time he was active in adult sports leagues and local politics. At holiday events he was always the life of the party.

But he was a different man at home—introverted, reclusive. After returning from school or football practice, he disappeared into his room with a book and a glass of chocolate milk and stayed there all evening. His kids didn't understand his split personality until he woke the whole house one night after Jim was already away at college. He was raving in his bed, babbling about bugs crawling all over him. Kelly and Lee raced to their parents' bedroom.

"Never mind. It's a bad dream," their mother said, blocking the doorway.

"Why won't he wake up?" Lee asked, peering past.

"What's wrong with him?" Kelly asked.

The din of his screaming reached a fever pitch, and Mrs. McIntyre closed the door behind her. She led the girls to the living room, away from the wails. They sat in pajamas on the couch. "Your father . . . drinks. Too much. And sometimes . . . this happens. He'll be fine tomorrow."

And he *was* fine the next morning. But after school that day, he mixed up his usual glass of brown milk. Kelly realized it was cut with scotch, not chocolate syrup. Milk for his growing stomach ulcers, whisky for his addiction. Mr. Mac was the picture of professionalism at work, while he slowly deteriorated at home.

Whenever Kelly watched her dad read books with Colin, jealousy flashed inside her for just a moment, followed by sympathy for her dad, who was making the most of this second chance—to be the attentive father he hadn't been to his own kids. After several bouts of rehab, he was now more sober than drunk, but his body had endured years of poisoning. He had to stop playing sports when he retired. He couldn't even play golf and rarely drove a car. Counseling and AA had beaten back his alcoholism enough to heal the ulcers in his stomach, but he never quit smoking unfiltered Kools, even after he was diagnosed with emphysema. He was too proud to use a walker, cane, or oxygen tank, and some foods made him gag, but he wouldn't admit it.

Kelly resented him for his refusal to take better care of his health. His condition worsened, and she felt herself pulling away emotionally, steeling her heart against the inevitable. But Colin was nine years old and needed his grandpa, so they visited often.

One night in September, they met at a restaurant for dinner. Kelly sat beside her mom and opposite her dad, who sat next to Colin. Her father looked tragically old. His black hair was still thick but graying at the temples. Wire-rimmed bifocals rested on his nose, the elegant gold matching the pocket watch he always carried. He wore a dress shirt and fitted sweater, his bowling-ball potbelly incongruous with his tall, spare frame. His skin looked much older than sixty-six years. A network of damaged capillaries mapped the atlas of his face, charting his long course of self-destruction. Every broken blood vessel reminded Kelly of the times she had seen him vomit shocking amounts of blood. She didn't hear the term "esophageal hemorrhages" until she was at college.

He ate the garlic bread that came with his lasagna, even though all four of them knew he would choke on it. He did. His rasping triggered a gag reflex, and his meal threatened to rise up.

"It's okay, Grandpa. Drink some water," Colin said.

"Dad, what can I do?"

"He's fine. He's fine," Kelly's mom said.

Mr. Mac got up to find a men's room. Kelly half-rose to help him, aware of all the eyes on them. Her mom grabbed her arm. "He's fine." The old man shambled toward the restrooms, a napkin to his mouth, his torso convulsing in a rhythmic contradiction of retching and swallowing. Everyone watched him shuffle across the dining room toward the privacy of a toilet stall, his dignity barely shielded by a paper-thin diner napkin.

On the drive home, tears trickled down Kelly's face. Colin patted her hand. "It's okay, Mom. Grandpa's just sick. He'll get better."

● ● ●

Later in September, Kelly spent the weekend on Long Island with her boyfriend. When the house phone rang at midnight, he said, "Don't answer it. It's my friends calling from their poker game." The answering machine picked up, and Kelly heard a tiny voice.

"Hi, Mom. It's me, Colin. I just wanted to let you know that Grandpa died." Kelly snatched the phone off its cradle.

"Hello, Colin, I'm here."

"Hi, Mom."

"Hey, Sweetie. Are you okay?"

"Yeah."

"Can I talk to Uncle Jim or Aunt Vicki?"

Colin passed the phone with a nine-year-old's partial understanding of the situation. He sat with his cousins while Jim told Kelly how their mom had found their dad in bed, called the ambulance, and attempted CPR. It was a heart attack, and he was gone.

The following days passed in a blur of tears, funeral arrangements, and neighbors' casseroles leading up to the wake in a small-town funeral home. Colin wore his chorus concert outfit, and Kelly dressed for mourning as they knelt together beside the open coffin. Colin's bright-blue eyes searched the coffin's satin bunting, traced the edge of his grandpa's suit coat, and followed the necktie to his serene face. "They should have cut his nose hairs," he said.

Kelly suppressed a laugh as the levity of the joke evaporated. "Do you want to kiss Grandpa good-bye?"

Colin nodded.

"Do you want me to go first?"

Colin nodded again.

Kelly leaned over and touched her lips to her dad's cheek. The temperature shocked her. "Be prepared," she said. "He's cold."

● ● ●

The wake lasted all day, and nobody in Kelly's family had time to sit down. Three and a half decades of former students and their families lined up at the door to pay their respects to Mr. Mac's wife and kids. People of all ages milled around in the parlor and commented on the photos, snapshots from his life. Mr. Mac's golf clubs stood beside his casket, blue-and-white knitted socks covering the drivers.

After the service, he was laid to rest in the cemetery near his home. Crowds stood silent under a steel-gray sky as the bagpipers played "Amazing Grace." For a moment, the sun broke through, and then it was gone.

FOUR O'CLOCK: Cynthia Raises the Stakes

Cynthia woke up and watched the striped curtains ripple in the languid breath of the ceiling fan. Her eyeballs ached, and her tongue felt mossy. Light leaked in below the curtains from the tropical sun, already high in the sky. She and Paul had been in the Dominican Republic for a week, staying at an all-inclusive resort.

Their hotel room was beautiful. Framed paintings hung on taupe walls. A couch, coffee table, and king-size bed furnished the room; French doors opened onto a balcony overlooking the pool. Granite tiles covered the bathroom walls and floor, but modern fixtures on that polished stone made it look futuristic, a space-age cave.

Cynthia looked around at the empty bottles of Red Stripe and *mamajuana* that cluttered the tabletops, trying to calculate how much she had drunk last night. She liked the sweet, earthy taste of the *mamajuana*, but the mystery of the herbs and bark attracted her more than the rum and wine they stewed in. The local people considered it a sort of witch's brew, able to cure all manner of problems. This was Cynthia's first trip outside the United States, and the concoction tasted like her experience felt: complex and alien, but deeply gratifying.

Working at the CVS photo counter in her blue polo shirt and white lab coat, she had developed countless passport pictures for people who were planning exotic vacations. She knew about Tahiti, Bora Bora, Puerto Rico, and the Bahamas. As soon as she and Paul had enough money, she booked this trip and went back to CVS with her passport application already filled out. She stapled her photos to the form while they were still warm.

Cynthia kept her pharmacy job but paid for this trip with her supplementary income from dealing pills. She also bought a car, a manual transmission VW CC VR6 sedan, fully loaded with heated leather seats and electronic everything. She talked to Paul's dad about it before she bought it, and he said it was a risk—it had 100,000 miles on it. That didn't dissuade her. She liked the dark red color. As soon as she bought it, she got rid of the roof rack and added a subwoofer that rattled the trunk. It was waiting for her in long-term parking at LaGuardia Airport, and she kind of missed it.

Cynthia thought about her car and their flight this afternoon. She was ready to go home. Riding dune buggies through the mud and paragliding over the ocean had been fun, but some of the excursions were creepy. The roofless hotel bus with its ratty canopy stopped at every little café for "authentic native dishes" and a photo op, followed by a sob story about the poverty of the local people. Every tourist had to cough up a donation before the driver started the engine, only to repeat the shakedown a few miles later. One young boy outside a sugarcane plantation sidled up to Cynthia and said "give me money," flashing his hooked farm blade. Paul tossed him five bucks.

The money poured out of their pockets all week, but Cynthia wasn't worried about it. Mrs. Ormand's prescription was due for a refill next week, so that was an easy grand. The tiny drug sample boxes had gotten her started, but prescription painkillers were more predictable and lucrative. Mrs. Ormand got three hundred pills a month, but nobody counts each pill in that huge bottle. Cynthia skimmed thirty off the top each month and sold them to a dealer. When Mrs. Ormand called in for her refill, they filled it even if it was a few days early. Cynthia had a dozen customers like that. And Paul had started buying sheets of LSD in Massachusetts to sell in Connecticut. They were both swimming in profits.

She spent her drug money on clothes, her car, and travel, but Paul spent his on cocaine. He didn't let Cynthia try it because he was afraid she'd get addicted. She sampled the painkillers instead. They filled her with manic energy and curiosity. Paul seemed to like her more that way, especially in bed. She tried everything, and she was insatiable.

But then Paul changed his opinion. He accused her of taking too many pills, eating into the profits. Whenever he caught her dosing, he forced her to have sex with him. Sometimes anal sex. Those experimental acts that had been their shared adventure in a sexual taboo, Paul now twisted into a cruel punishment. If he realized she was high on painkillers, he raped her.

Cynthia hadn't done any drugs for a while before their trip, and she felt closer to Paul than ever. Her foot slid under the covers to rest against his leg. Cynthia wanted to take another swim in the pool before they caught the shuttle to the airport, but her eyes hurt just thinking of the heat, the bright sun, and the oppressive humidity. She knew her head would ache when she stood up to start packing, so she just lay there watching the flutter of the curtain and waiting for Paul to stir.

FOUR O'CLOCK: **Trials**

At three o'clock, the hero crosses the threshold into the special world, and the following hour is filled with tests and challenges. At this point in Homer's *Odyssey*, Telemachus talks with his father's comrades, who tell him tales of Odysseus's clever heroics. Thinking his father lost at sea, Telemachus is overcome by grief at losing a father he has never known. Then, during his return voyage to Ithaca, he faces ambush by those who hope to wed his mother and thus seize his father's lands and property. Telemachus's emotions take him by surprise, just like his enemies plan to do on the ocean.

Meanwhile, after Odysseus survives a storm at sea, he washes up on unknown shores, where he's treated as an honored guest by the local king. During the royal feast, Odysseus describes the trials he endured after the Trojan War: the lotus-eaters, the cyclops Polyphemus, the witch Circe, the Sirens, and the deadly Scylla and Charybdis. His hosts are deeply impressed and offer their support for his return home. Although the narrative is not linear, this section of Odysseus's story relates the hero overcoming adversity.

Our contemporary adventure tales often follow the same pattern. After arriving at the Capitol, Katniss survives burns, venomous insects, and hand-to-hand combat in the early stages of The Hunger Games. Frodo Baggins overcomes various monsters and his own temptation as he progresses toward Mount Doom in *The Lord of the Rings* trilogy. These tests, challenges, and trials represent the fourth hour of the hero's journey cycle.

In *The Wonderful Wizard of Oz*, author L. Frank Baum modifies the monomyth formula to mingle the fourth stage, Trials, with the second stage, Assistance. Dorothy follows the yellow brick road, *then* helps the Scarecrow and invites him to accompany her to the Emerald City. The two use their wits to save the Tin Man from paralysis, and he befriends them. A lion attacks them all, and Dorothy scolds him. He submits, confessing his cowardice, and joins their quest to see the Wizard.

Cynthia's journey is no yellow brick road. After stealing drugs from her employer, she follows a darker path. No longer a recreational consumer of illegal drugs, she's now a distributor. Cynthia has become a felon, siphoning narcotics from legal medical channels into her own black market enterprise. Her illicit income buys a car and a Caribbean vacation, but she spends every day worrying about getting caught. The stress takes its toll, and she starts popping pills herself, hoping to control her anxiety. Meanwhile, Paul's cocaine habit changes his personality and their relationship. He becomes more controlling and domineering. Their love life had always been another expression of their adventurous spirits, but Paul twists their intimacy into one-sided sadistic violence. Cynthia finds herself on the dark side, uncertain what's next.

At three o'clock in the monomyth cycle, Colin became aware that his family tree was missing a major limb. At four o'clock, Colin faces trials in this strange new territory. He starts to understand the cruel comments he overhears, but those barbs don't compare to the shockwave caused by his grandfather's death. Propped up by his mom, he soldiers on.

The heroes of the original *Star Wars* movie are also waylaid shortly after departing on their journey. Their spaceship is trapped and the droids are captured. Using their wits and the Force, Han Solo and Luke Skywalker rescue Princess Leia and escape in the *Millennium Falcon*, but Obi-Wan falls at Darth Vader's hand. The next time Colin slept over at his grandma's house, he watched that scene and knew just how helpless and alone Luke felt at that moment.

Recall the book or movie you identified in chapter three. If your hero set off on a physical or emotional journey, what happened next in the plot? If the journey was smooth, there would be no story. Surely there was some complication—that would be considered a Trial in terms of the monomyth cycle. Does this formula also apply to an episode in your own personal history? Think of the obstacles you met in the special world that you ventured into at the end of chapter three. (If you passed through that unfamiliar territory without encountering any curveballs, then try to remember a journey that was a little more heroic.) Like Dorothy or Luke, you probably had to do some quick thinking in this new landscape. What were those Trials you faced?

What about your teenagers? Are they navigating a strange new world? Perhaps they are learning the ropes at a new school, or just dealing with changes in their own bodies. They are certainly managing interpersonal dynamics, the rules of which can change suddenly, thrusting an unsuspecting teenager into the uncharted territory of love triangles or friendship rivalries. This is when they need Assistance from their wise mentor—you.

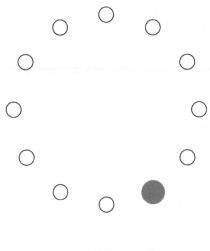

CHAPTER 5

Approach

T he die is cast. The moment of truth approaches. During this fifth hour of the cycle, our hero prepares himself or herself for a reckoning. Henry V rallies his men for battle on St. Crispin's Day. The gunfighter gathers his courage for a showdown at high noon. Luke Skywalker fuels his X-wing fighter for the assault on the Death Star,", but Han Solo walks away.

FIVE O'CLOCK: **Colin Stakes His Claim**

After Colin finished his homework, he searched the refrigerator for a snack. Kelly hugged him from behind. He was growing so fast, but Colin's energetic personality had faded in the weeks since his grandfather's funeral. "Why don't you make a list of the things you'd like for Christmas?" she said. Kelly couldn't buy fancy gifts with her housekeeping income and welfare checks. Colin was lucky to get new sweatpants and a box of Cap'n Crunch for his birthday, but each

Christmas, Colin's aunt, uncle, and grandparents divided up his wish list and did their best to spoil him.

Colin closed the fridge and turned into her. "I don't want any presents," he said, his voice muffled as he hugged her. "But would you please find my dad?"

Both of them froze when the words fell from his mouth. Then Kelly leaned back to study her son's face. Colin's expression shifted from uncertainty to regret. Kelly knew that her own feelings had betrayed her.

She hugged him close again, trying to swallow her fear. "That's what you want?" Colin nodded into her chest.

Kelly had buried that shame long ago, and it was terrifying to exhume. Why had she waited so long? When she returned from the hospital after giving birth to Colin, Kelly received a letter from Bill, her ex-boyfriend. He explained that he'd been diagnosed with violent schizophrenia soon after they split up and was living in a mental institution. He had learned about her pregnancy and assumed he was responsible. At the time, Kelly wasn't sure what to make of this bizarre piece of news. She'd already settled on single motherhood, so she decided to ignore the letter. The situation was complicated enough without adding a violent schizophrenic.

Over time, she questioned her decision. When Colin turned two years old, she spoke to a lawyer and learned the ABCs of establishing paternity: a long, degrading process of legal summonses, blood tests, and affidavits. *Oh my God*, she thought, *I can't do that.* Kelly couldn't bear to publicly admit Colin's uncertain paternity. Her parents still didn't know, and they would certainly find out if the courts got involved. And the lawyer's attitude was so heartless. It was all about how much money Kelly was entitled to, but that wasn't her motivation at all. The whole process was too overwhelming, so she dropped it.

Years later, when Colin joined the first-grade soccer league, she had to present his birth certificate to sign up. The space for "Father" was filled with "---------." Mortified, Kelly spoke to another lawyer about adding a name, but she still could not bear the humiliation of contacting both potential fathers and revisiting that lost, brazen weekend. She prayed obsessively for the courage to make those phone calls but never found it. Instead, she held out hope that the past would never catch up with her—that Colin might pass his whole life without wanting to resolve that mystery.

But with this Christmas request, Kelly knew her day of reckoning had finally dawned. This question was in her son's way, and only she had the power to remove it. Standing in their kitchen, looking into his grieving blue eyes, she said the only thing she could say. "Of course I will." She stroked his hair and held him. "Of course I will."

●   ●   ●

After Colin went to school the next day, Kelly reached for the phonebook and opened it to the page she had flagged the night before. She dialed Bill's parents' house, expecting to leave a message. Bill's mother answered the phone.

"Hello?"

"Um, hello. My name is Kelly McIntyre, and I'm an old friend of Bill's. We've fallen out of touch, and I'm trying to contact him. Would you be willing to give me his number or take my number down?" Just like she rehearsed.

"Well, actually, he lives here with us. Why don't you leave me your number."

Kelly waited anxiously for days, but didn't tell Colin anything. When the house phone rang three nights later, she answered hesitantly.

"Hello?"

"Hi, this is Bill. I'm calling for Kelly."

"Hi, um, give me a second." Kelly stretched the curling green phone wire all the way into the bathroom and closed the door. Colin noticed. "Thanks for calling me back," she said, quietly.

"No. Thanks for your call. Really." A pregnant pause. "You know, Kelly, all this time I've wondered. I always wanted to pick up the phone too. I'm glad that you found the courage, because I never did."

"Yeah, well, it only took me nine years. So, I guess I should tell you why I called you now, out of the blue." And she confessed the tale of that long-ago May weekend, the fickle heart of a reckless young woman she no longer knew. "Bill, you owe me nothing, but if you're willing, the next step would be DNA testing. I would pay for it, but they're only open during the week, so you might miss work."

"You know, I always liked the idea that there was a boy out there who might be my son. Yeah. Sure, I'll do the test."

"Thank you, Bill. I really appreciate this. I'll get some dates from them and call you tomorrow."

"Okay. Good. I'll talk to you tomorrow. Good night."

Kelly listened to the click, then the silence. She leaned against the bathroom wall, thinking about the blood test, coming to a kind of awareness of that fluid racing through her body. It felt so thin, so light. She was so close now, so close to giving Colin the answer he needed.

Later that night, over carrots and homemade chicken nuggets, Kelly told Colin, "I spoke with Bill, and he's agreed to find out if he's the father. So the next step is that we'll all go to Albany to give blood samples. And then the lab will be able to tell if Bill is your father."

Colin stood up from the table, crossed to his mom, and hugged her in silence. It felt good to give him what he wanted, and she hoped that she was. But what if Bill wasn't Colin's father? What would Kelly do then? She tamped down her own anxiety and suspense, controlling her voice to say, "Listen now. Don't get your hopes up. This doesn't mean he's the one, so . . . just hold on until we get the results."

●   ●   ●

A month later, they drove up to the GenTech offices in Albany. Mother and son entered a nondescript building and walked into what felt like a dentist's office. A female doctor in a business suit led them to a private room to draw their blood. Kelly sat down in the modified reclining chair and showed Colin that it didn't hurt. When it was his turn, Colin jumped into the seat and laid his arm on the sterile armrest. He watched as the needle entered his vein.

"You can look away," the doctor assured him.

"No, it's okay." The plunger retracted and bright-red blood filled the cylinder. His jaw clenched, but Colin didn't cry.

Afterward they went to the Colonie Mall, where Bill was waiting in the food court. "Hi," Kelly said. They hugged hello.

Bill adjusted his shirt. "Kelly, thanks for doing this."

Kelly nodded a smile. Bill looked down at Colin and gave him a grin. "I've heard a lot about you," he said. Colin peered up at him.

"Go ahead. I'll wait right here," Kelly said.

Bill turned toward the shops and Colin followed beside him. They walked slowly, falling into a comfortable pace.

"So, what grade are you in?"

"Second grade. I go to Pine Tree. I have Mrs. Davis."

"Oh, yeah? How do you like school? What's your favorite subject?"

"I like math and gym. Math is easy for me. I'm kind of a genius."

"Wow. Do you play any sports?"

"All of 'em. You know, at recess and stuff. I like running. I'm pretty fast."

They walked past a video arcade, Spencer's Gifts, and the Orange Julius. They talked for an hour. Kelly was waiting near the Cinnabon when they returned. It almost seemed normal.

She stood up. "OK, well . . . maybe we'll do this again sometime," she said.

"Yeah, I hope so," Bill said.

Kelly gave Bill a hug. Colin shook his hand.

Mother and son walked outside and Kelly started their beat-up Honda. Colin sat very still during the long ride south. He was looking out the window, out over the snowy shoulder of the Thruway, over the deer fences, through the bare trees at the glowing yellow windows of the occasional houses floating by in the settling dusk.

"Are you okay?" Kelly asked.

"I hope it's him." Colin said. Kelly put her hand on his knee.

● ● ●

The days followed in rarified suspense. Colin got off the bus and checked the mailbox. Nothing from GenTech. Somewhere the scientists were decoding his blood. He finished his homework and played Nintendo; he had to keep busy. He kept thinking about that day, just walking around the mall with his dad—or maybe his dad. *Wouldn't it be awesome if we could do that all the time?* he thought. More mail came every day, but it held no news.

One night Colin was sitting on the overstuffed, threadbare couch and playing Duck Hunt on their hand-me-down TV. Kelly watched him for a while from the kitchen table. When his game was over, she said, "Come over here." Colin looked over at her and dropped the plastic gun onto the carpet.

"Did you find out?"

Kelly nodded, holding the GenTech letter in her hands.

"What does it say? Is Bill my dad?"

She showed him the results. His eyes scanned the page and stopped at the all-caps line at the bottom. His expression changed, and Kelly hugged him to her chest.

THIS CANDIDATE IS EXCLUDED.

FIVE O'CLOCK: **Cynthia Sees What's Coming**

Paul was freaking out, and Cynthia thought he might die in her arms. They were in the toy aisle of Stop & Shop, their favorite place to go when they were rolling on E, to play with the colorful squirt guns and Nerf balls. They had both taken a lot of Ecstasy, but Paul soon moved beyond tripping. His head lolled on his neck, and his eyes were rolling back in his head. Cynthia tried to snap him out of it, but he just mumbled and grabbed at her arms.

She called their friend Dave to ask him what to do.

"What are you doing?" Paul said and grabbed at the phone.

"I'm calling Dave. I'm worried about you."

"Who are you calling? Are you calling the cops on me?" He tried to rip the phone out of her hand.

"Stop it! You're tripping balls."

"I'm fine! Don't call the cops!" Paul grabbed her arm and squeezed, hard.

"Stop, Paul! You're hurting me!"

His eyes bulged and he swooned again. Cynthia snapped her phone free and thumbed Dave's number, propping Paul up with her other arm. He babbled about shampoo while Cynthia explained the situation into the phone.

"Go buy some orange juice so he'll roll harder," Dave said.

"I'm serious, Dave. He's really scaring me."

"Meet me outside in ten minutes. We'll drive around until he mellows out."

Cynthia hung up and shuffled Paul toward the cash registers, his arm around her neck. She was also high, but too scared to enjoy it. She overlooked the vibrant colors, repressed the feelings of euphoria. They had taken around twenty-five pills over the last two days, and everything had been going great until about an hour ago. Cynthia had woken up in her bedroom to the sound of Paul pounding on something. She had found him trapped in her closet, covered in tinfoil and screaming that he was lost. When she opened the closet door, Paul tumbled out, tangled in a knot of dresses. Cynthia had hustled him out of the house before her mom could ask any questions.

● ● ●

Dave picked them up in front of Stop & Shop, and they drove down the Miracle Mile, store lights winking on under a darkening sky. "Whoa! Look out for the dogs!" Paul screamed. There were no dogs. "Check out all the Barbie balls."

Dave laughed, but Cynthia didn't. "He keeps saying that."

"He's tripping out. Are you sure he's only on E? What else did you take, Paul?" Dave asked.

Paul just stared out the window, mesmerized. Cynthia watched his eyelids flutter over his unnaturally black eyes, his pupils hyperdilated. Whenever she saw the whites of his eyes slide up, she shook him. "Paul!" They drove for hours like this, and she swore they would stop doing this, stop partying, stop pushing their luck.

Cynthia quit stealing from the pharmacy after they got back from the Dominican Republic. She got a car and a vacation out of it, but was afraid of getting caught. Paul had other plans anyway. When his parents were out of town, he and Cynthia opened up the box he'd ordered online. They put on rubber gloves and surgical masks and mixed ingredients in the kitchen.

Paul's brother walked in. "What are you doing? Are you cooking crack? You'd better not be cooking crack."

"No, we're making pizza." Paul said.

"I know you're not fucking making pizza."

They mixed the spores according to the instructions, but Paul cultivated the mushrooms in secret and hid the leathery buttons from Cynthia. He wouldn't let her try them because he wanted to sell them, but sometimes she noticed his dazed expression, and Paul confessed to eating them alone. It didn't seem fair that he held all the cards.

One summer afternoon at Paul's house, Cynthia started to hallucinate but couldn't figure out why. She'd heard that LSD could stay in your spinal fluid and seep out later, causing unexpected acid trips. Everything looked like bright light. She lay on the floor with her eyes closed but couldn't stop her racing brain. *What's going on? Am I dying? If I'm dying, I really like dying. I don't know why I keep thinking in my head. Why do I keep thinking in my head? Why am I not talking?*

"What's wrong?" Paul asked.

"I don't know," Cynthia said.

"Are you drunk? Did you drink?"

"No."

"Are you rolling? Did you drop some E?"

"No."

"Are you tripping?"

"No."

"Ha! Yeah, you are!" Paul said. "I dosed your sandwich!"

"What?" This confused Cynthia even more. Why would he spike her food? Paul was laughing, but Cynthia was just trying to catch up to what was happening. She spent the next few hours feeling slightly nauseated, continuing that mental dialogue with herself but feeling guarded at the same time. She had always known Paul was unpredictable, but she thought she was exempt as a target. From then on, she couldn't help wondering what he might do next.

Paul continued to experiment with mushrooms and other drugs while dealing more acid and Ecstasy. One of their painkillers customers was a dealer who traveled around with music shows. He put them in touch with his source for E, and the rest was easy. They drove up to Massachusetts and bought a hundred pills at three dollars each. They had a monopoly on the local Ecstasy market, reselling the pills for twenty bucks a pop. With such huge profits, they could afford to sample the merchandise.

But lately it was getting out of control. Last time, they drove home with a sheet of 100 tabs of LSD and about 500 tablets of ecstasy. The latest version of Ecstasy had the head of Optimus Prime stamped into it. The pill really was a transformer—much more potent than Gs up, hoes down.

● ● ●

Dave dropped them off at Paul's house in the early morning, after his dad had already left for his graveyard shift at the factory. They both collapsed in Paul's bedroom and slept all day. Paul seemed fine when they woke up.

"Are you sure you're okay?" Cynthia asked.

"Yeah."

"You scared the shit out of me. Your eyes were rolling around. I thought you were dying."

"I'm fine."

"We've got to stop that, okay? I can't handle it."

"Yeah. Let's just cut it out for a while," Paul said.

Cynthia followed through on that pledge, slogging through the fatigue and depression of withdrawal over the next few days. The hours at work passed in a fog, and the remains of the day were bleak and flat. She lost her appetite. She heard somber undertones in even the most upbeat techno songs. Sleep hung above her but wouldn't settle on her eyes, taunting her with exhaustion but no relief. Not even snuggling with Mr. Peabody, her pet rabbit, cheered her up.

Cynthia wanted to take the edge off, just a little something to pull her out of the funk, not to get high. She resisted that temptation but could never tell if Paul was sneaking hits from some private stash.

Her energy and appetite returned within a week or two, but Cynthia's stomach didn't follow suit. She couldn't keep any food down. The doctor put her on a special diet, and she stuck to it, hoping to avoid a rerun of her disastrous year at Pace. Cynthia lived on slices of white bread, thinly spread with real butter. Her hunger reached out to the smells around her—the rich, smoky aroma of peanuts, the greasy heat of french fries—but she didn't dare put anything in her mouth. She knew her stomach would flip everything out again, so she ate only bread and hoped the illness would pass.

Cynthia and Paul both looked much healthier during his family's annual vacation to Cape Cod. This year, Paul's mom and her siblings rented a rambling old house with classic cedar-shake siding and a wood-shingle roof. Paul's Aunt Katherine and her husband came with their two preteen kids. His Aunt Darleen brought her two little white dogs, a terrier and something like a Shih Tzu. There were four bedrooms and one bathroom upstairs, all filled with aunts, uncles, and kids, so Cynthia and Paul slept on an air mattress in the finished basement beside a couple of arcade games from the 1980s. At least they had their own bathroom.

During the day they went to beaches, water parks, and minigolf courses. They even drove go-carts with Paul's dad, cousins, and uncle. Everyone jockeyed for position and hugged the inside corner until Paul's ten-year-old cousin took the checkered flag. In the evening they swam in the backyard pool while salmon and steak cooked on the grill. It smelled delicious. After dinner each night they drove to a local farm that served handmade ice cream. Cynthia ate every flavor with her eyes, but couldn't take a bite.

Cynthia was glad that Paul's dad came. He was a loner and worked odd hours to avoid dealing with people. He wore sweatpants and a T-shirt to his factory shift from three o'clock in the morning to one o'clock in the afternoon, and he went to bed right after dinner. He was tall and lean, with salt-and-pepper gray hair and a sarcastic attitude. He'd been an alcoholic until ten years earlier, when he quit after his wife's liver transplant. Now he always got upset when Paul drank too much.

Paul's mom was his counterpoint. She almost died from that liver transplant and her stomach never healed right, but she kept up with her full-time job at the town library and always seemed to a have something baking in the kitchen. She was almost as tall as her husband and built like a Viking, but her hair was black and curly. She wore khaki slacks with turtleneck shirts and comfortable shoes. She always marveled at how Cynthia could walk around in high heels.

One afternoon Paul and his mom drove Cynthia to a surprise destination. She knew it was the anniversary of their first date, but she was surprised Paul remembered. He told her to wear sensible clothes, so she wore a T-shirt, shorts, and high heels. Paul's mom packed her sneakers and drove them to a wide-open part of Cape Cod.

"Are we going to the beach?"

"Yup, yup." Paul said. They turned up a road, and Cynthia saw orange cones lined up to an airplane in an empty field.

"Is this an airport? We're going skydiving!"

"No shit!" Paul said.

They stopped in front of the camper that served as a temporary office. A short man with a moustache greeted them in broken English and helped them both climb into parachutes. He walked them over to the rickety plane and introduced the pilot and the two skydivers who would tandem-jump with them. It was hard to understand what they were saying. Paul's mom took pictures and laughed.

"Smile, you crazy kids!"

Cynthia and Paul ducked their heads and sat on the laps of the skydivers as the plane sped bouncing down the ratty grass strip, engine noise filling the open cabin and jarring the seats. Wind blasted in through the empty doorframes as they lifted off.

"What happens if I change my mind?" Cynthia said, shouting to be heard.

"You go!" her skydiver said, pointing at the receding landscape with a smile.

Paul screamed suddenly and was gone. There was an empty seat next to her. She felt a hand on her ankle.

"Here," her partner positioned her foot on the doorframe. "Okay?"

Before she could reply, she was trapped inside a tumbling wave. Rushing air suffocated her voice, weightlessness flared in her stomach, fear tugged at her bladder. The cocktail of disorientation, exhilaration, and alarm reminded her of tripping on acid, but this was much more real. Then she was floating still, hanging upright from her partner and drifting above the world, the crooked arm of Cape Cod stretched out below, the dark bay flecked with white. It was the most beautiful thing she'd ever seen.

FIVE O'CLOCK: **Approach**

After overcoming the initial trials, the hero zeros in on the object of his or her quest. The fifth stage, the Approach, represents that hour before the reckoning. The gunfighter checks his ammunition. Daedalus reminds Icarus not to fly too close to the sun. Frodo passes through the lair of a giant spider on his way to Mount Doom. The Wicked Witch of the West waylays Dorothy and her friends in a field of poppies. All heroes recognize the peril of the situation at this stage, but they proceed nevertheless.

Many stories use this moment to build suspense, reminding readers of what hangs in the balance and the difficulty of the hero's task. In Homer's *Odyssey*, the parallel plotlines of Telemachus and Odysseus finally come together when they reunite. Along with Odysseus's loyal servants, father and son plot an attack on the presumptuous suitors encamped in the great hall of their home. They are heavily outnumbered, but their cause is just, much like in the original *Star Wars* movie, when the rebels coordinate their assault on the Death Star. Luke loads up his X-wing fighter for the dangerous mission, but Han Solo begs off. Katniss Everdeen has spent much of the Hunger Games evading her enemies, but she prepares to confront them as time runs short.

Our heroes tend to attain what they pursued after battling through interesting complications. Rarely do they achieve the prize only to watch it evaporate before their eyes, leaving them empty-handed. That is Colin's experience at five o'clock in the cycle. He believes he has found the answer to the central question of his life, and the solution to his poverty. Sadly, Bill turns out to be a false trail on Colin's journey.

In a similar way, Cynthia probably thought that the moment in the toy aisle at Stop & Shop was six o'clock, and that she and Paul were now on the upswing, both transformed by that terrifying experience. She might have been right. If they had both stayed on the straight and narrow path, they might have returned to the ordinary world of sober, law-abiding citizens, and Cynthia's story would have a different shape. In hindsight, Paul's overdose was not a turning point but merely a prelude to a bigger crisis.

Think of the pivotal moments in your life. Did you see them coming? What led up to them? Did you anticipate a clincher that didn't occur, as Colin did? Or did you credit a turning point that turned out to be another leg in a longer journey, like Cynthia?

Consider the teens in your life. Each is on a journey to his or her next defining moment. Some of them can see it coming: the championship game, the prom, or the college admissions letter. Others can't put a finger on it or mark it on the calendar, but it looms on the horizon like a thunderhead. And they are headed straight for it.

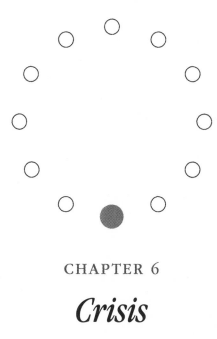

CHAPTER 6

Crisis

S ix o'clock is the turning point, when the hero faces his or her greatest fear. At this moment the hero dies (literally or symbolically) and is replaced by a more powerful version. Theseus slays the Minotaur. Odin is crucified on the World Tree. Luke Skywalker trusts his feelings, uses the Force, and destroys the Death Star.

SIX O'CLOCK: **Colin's Moment of Truth**

Kelly had hoped Bill was the one. They'd grown up in the same town, dated for eight months during college, and he seemed genuinely interested in Colin. There was no help for it. Tim must be Colin's biological father. A one-night stand, a man she hardly knew. And Kelly had no clue where he was or how to find him.

Ten years ago they'd attended Eisenhower College together. Tim was a senior and Kelly was a freshman when the college went bankrupt and stopped admitting new students. Three years later, Kelly's cohort was the last to graduate before the college closed its doors forever. Kelly didn't know how to get in touch with any of her class-mates, but she knew someone who would.

Along with Adult Children of Alcoholics and Al-Anon meetings, Kelly usually joined the Saturday-morning AA group at her church. She'd ended her wild partying a decade earlier, but fear of sliding into her dad's footsteps kept her attending twelve-step meetings. Everyone usually walked to the local diner afterward, and that's when Kelly approached Tom, a retired cop from the Bronx who now worked as a limo driver and private detective. In the parking lot, Kelly told him that she was looking for her son's father. Kelly was just hoping for advice, but Tom said, "Give me what you have; I'll look into it for you."

● ● ●

Tom called Kelly on Monday. "I found him. Yeah, he's in Middletown."

Kelly couldn't speak. All this time, all eleven years of Colin's life, Tim had been living just twenty minutes away. She might have bumped into him at Shop Rite.

"What did . . . how did you . . . ?"

"I looked his name up in the phone book, figuring I might find a relative. I called a few numbers and told 'em I was organizing a reunion for Eisenhower College, class of 1980. He picked up on the third call. I got lucky." Kelly took a deep breath. "He's married, two kids, runs a day care. Got a house on Highland Avenue. You want the address?"

Kelly fished out a pen and wrote it down, stunned. She couldn't process this. It was so unexpected, so sudden. And a family. A complete family unit. He seemed even more untouchable now, like his family existed on some higher social plane. She knew the majestic homes that lined Highland Avenue, imposing colonial houses from the turn of the twentieth century and the pride of historic Middletown. Tim's family lived in a Norman Rockwell paradise, and Kelly would have to smash it to fulfill Colin's Christmas wish. That seemed impossible.

Kelly knew how it would look. A welfare mom knocks on the door with her eleven-year-old child in tow, talking about a one-night stand in 1982. Kelly would be labeled a home wrecker. His wife would accuse her of slander. Tim was a family man now, a productive member of society. How would he react when the claim inevitably proved true? How would his wife react? Would they divorce? Would his children look at their father differently? Would they despise him? Kelly couldn't accept the responsibility for so much destruction.

She wrestled with the information for six months, trying to come up with a way to give Colin what he needed without injuring Tim's family. Finally she drove to their house, just to look at it. Maybe that would inspire a solution to this impasse. She got off the highway, drove past shopping centers and strip malls, down the crumbling antique main street to Tim's neighborhood, a tribute to the town's proud history. She parked in front of the house, a beautiful Victorian home with elaborate gardens, immaculately kept. Kelly peered through her car window like it was a television screen. The house hardly seemed real.

* * *

Twenty minutes later, Kelly pulled into her parking spot and descended the concrete steps to her shabby bungalow. She stopped in the front yard and looked at it with fresh eyes. She and Colin lived in a house that would fit inside Tim's garage. She dismissed the thought and walked to the screen door, but the imbalance struck her again as soon as she entered. Everything her eyes touched reminded her of their poverty: the cast-off sofa, the garage sale–modern coffee table, the hand-me-down dish set, the mottled carpeting from another decade, and Colin's sneakers beside the door, a contribution from last year's People for People fund at her church.

Wait a minute, she thought. *Wait a minute. Wait a minute. I'm caring more about his family than I am about my own.* Something that a lawyer had said nine years earlier popped into her head. Kelly had asked an attorney named Carol Klein to establish paternity but explained that she didn't want to petition for child support. No money, just a name on the birth certificate.

"That's not your decision to make." Carol had said. "That money doesn't belong to you. It belongs to your child, and your child is entitled."

Kelly blinked. "I just want to establish the facts. I'm not after money."

"It's not up to you. Colin is owed this money. I can help you change his birth certificate, but I will also make sure that Colin's father provides support according to the law."

Kelly couldn't sign up for that, so Carol had refused to take the case. Finally, nine years later, Kelly understood Carol's point. She reached for the phone and called the state department of social services. The social worker listened carefully to Kelly's story and engaged the legal machinery. Within a few weeks, Tim received a certified letter from the Family Court of Orange County.

• • •

A few months later, Kelly stood beside a state lawyer in the Orange County Family Court, with Tim across the aisle beside his own counsel. He still had his trim moustache from ten years ago, along with the same youthful twinkle in his eye. Kelly couldn't help noticing that Colin was already taller than him. He denied paternity, so the judge ordered blood tests and struck the gavel. Outside in the parking lot, Tim walked up to Kelly.

"Can I talk to you?"

"Sure," Kelly said.

"It's been a really long time since I've seen you, but I remember that night."

Kelly felt goose skin rise on her neck.

"Listen, I'm still trying to get my head around all this," Tim said.

"I'm sure it's quite a surprise."

"If it turns out that I'm—"

"You are. It's you."

Tim's shoulders sagged a little. He took a breath. "Well, I hope that my heart is big enough to do the right thing." Almost to himself, he added, "but I don't know if it is."

• • •

From then on, everywhere she and Colin went, Kelly worried that they might bump into Tim. She avoided McDonald's and the diner. When Colin had his all-county chorus recital in Goshen, Kelly ducked her head and scanned the audience. She and Colin submitted more blood tests and waited for updates from the court. As time passed, Kelly's anxiety increased. What was happening inside Tim's house? He must have gotten his blood test results by now and learned the truth. Had he accepted it? Had he told his wife? Would he want visitation rights, or did he have an even bigger agenda? Kelly imagined Tim and his wife suing for custody of Colin and adding him to their ideal family. They could point to Kelly's poverty and her history of mental illness. How could she fight back? She couldn't outspend them on lawyers. They could take Colin away from her if they wanted to. The fear grew inside her for eight months while the gears of family court slowly turned.

Finally a letter arrived with the date for another hearing. Kelly's lawyer explained that a judge would read the DNA results into the court record, and Tim would be declared Colin's father in the eyes of the law. He would become responsible for monthly child support payments, and Colin's birth certificate would be reprinted with Tim's name on it.

Beyond that, Kelly had no idea what might happen.

●　●　●

On that day, Colin sat in a plastic chair in the busy waiting room of the Orange County Family Court. He was five-foot-nine and gangly, and his best jeans only reached his shins. He wore a clean T-shirt over his lean frame, his arms folded over it. His bright-red, bowl-cut hair lay flat against his round head, which he held rigid with attention. His blue eyes were focused on the door at the far end of the room. It was closed.

Beside him sat his Aunt Lee. Her dark hair ended below her jawline but exposed the nape of her neck. Her clothes seemed too dressy to wear with white sneakers, but that was her habit. Other people were seated nearby—some with kids, some without. Colin didn't notice them. He was watching the door that his mom had gone through. He knew who else was behind it: his dad. When he made mischief at school, he knew what the teachers said. "What do you expect? He's got no father." On top of that social stigma was the life-style gap. Other kids had better sneakers, newer winter coats, and the latest video games. If he and his mom had a second income—a dad's income—he could have that stuff too.

And why didn't they have a dad's income? Simply because his dad didn't know of Colin's existence. It all seemed so simple. If he simply knew that he had a son, wouldn't he be excited? Wouldn't he want his son to have a good life? Colin stared at the wooden door as if his gaze could burn through it. It swung open and his mom walked out.

His aunt stood up, blocking his view. Colin dodged around her, but the clerk had already announced more names. People crossed the waiting room. Colin searched from face to face for the man in the snapshot his mom had shown him last night—the wavy blond hair, the moustache. He would be coming this way. Would they hug or shake hands?

Then he felt his mom's arm around him.

Colin looked at her. "Where is he?"

"That's him," she said, pointing.

Colin peered through the crowd and could make out the back of Tim's head as he left the building.

SIX O'CLOCK: **Cynthia's Last Straw**

It was a perfect summer Saturday when they pulled into the parking lot of Six Flags Great Adventure. The sky stretched out above them, a hazy blue. Paul rolled his silver Civic to a standstill in a remote cor-ner of the asphalt field. The journey had taken three hours with the long toll lines on the New Jersey Turnpike, but the Wild Safari drive was worth the trip. They both tipped their seats back and stared up at the empty sky, bathing in the air-conditioning.

"Can you believe that monkey? I thought he was gonna pull that car's door off!"

"That was funny."

"Glad he didn't try that on my car."

They deserved this day of fun. Paul was working hard at the Tractor Supply Company and commuting to the University of Connecticut (UConn) in Waterbury. Cynthia rode with him to campus and did her homework in the car until he could drop her at Naugatuck Community College. She carpooled home with her brother, who took classes there too. They were still dealing a little on the side, but only to steady customers. They were doing the right things, moving forward.

"I liked the giraffe. We should go back sometime."

"Definitely," Cynthia said.

Paul tipped his seat up and opened a pack of grape-flavored cigars and a bag of pot. With a delicate and practiced hand, he fashioned a blunt from the cigar's outer leaf. Cynthia rolled her head on her neck. They had dosed before entering the safari, so the five tabs of acid and one hit of Ecstasy were starting to kick in. The gray interior of the car seemed slightly unusual in color and texture.

"Let's take another star. They aren't as badass as everyone says." Paul lit the blunt and took a deep drag. Cynthia reached for the orange juice and then remembered Paul's bad trip with the Transformer pills. These new star-shaped pills had an even worse reputation, but what harm could a second tablet do? One hit of E had no effect on either of them anymore. She handed the OJ bottle to Paul and took the cigar in exchange. He tossed back a star and chased it with juice. Cynthia held the smoke in her lungs as long as she could and then popped a second pill too.

When the second cigar was smoked to ashes, they followed the yellow-and-red cement barriers that split the parking lot. They looked like giant blocks of candy lined up end to end, leading to the main gate. Behind the ticket booths, colorful ribbons of steel swept up into the sky. Muted, distant screams washed over them in waves.

"I gotta piss." Paul said. He walked toward the men's room, a blue door in the maroon cinderblock wall beside the front gate. Cynthia stood in the shade waiting for him. Her flip-flops warmed with the heat of the sidewalk, and she could feel the seams of her bikini under her T-shirt and shorts. She felt for her phone but remembered it was in the car. The computer-printed day passes were in Paul's pocket. *I can't wait to ride that water slide,* she thought, just starting to feel blissful.

"CYNTHIA!" Paul burst out of the men's room. "Cynthia! Run!" Paul grabbed her wrist as he bolted toward the parking lot. Cynthia raced to keep up with him, her flip-flops twisting from her toes.

"What? What's wrong?"

"Run! They're gonna rape you!" They fled like deer.

Someone in a uniform noticed them and jogged to intercept. Paul accelerated. Cynthia lost a sandal and kicked the other one off, sprinting now like a college soccer star. They dodged around cars and ran out of the parking lot, turning onto the empty road.

"Paul—slow down!" Cynthia dragged behind him, concentrating on her bare feet and watching for broken glass on the hot tarmac. "What did you see back there?"

Paul didn't slow down. Between breaths he said, "I saw them . . . in the bathroom . . . raping . . . a girl . . . not safe . . . they've got guns . . . run!"

Cynthia felt her panic rise past sober reason. The trees along the road seemed to darken, to move with sinister intent. She glanced back. Was that car chasing them? She ignored the scalding pavement, slapping her bare feet down the road toward escape.

They ran blindly, frantically, sure of a threat but unsure of any safe direction. They ran like rabbits that smell a fox but don't see it. Another mile at a breakneck pace.

"Stop—Paul—stop."

Paul didn't stop.

"My feet—stop." Cynthia broke free of his grip and staggered to sit down on the shoulder of the road. Her feet were bleeding. She studied the soles, picked out gravel, bits of glass. Paul squatted next to her, frantic. He looked back up the road, expecting Armageddon.

"Come on! Let's go!" he said.

"Paul, I can't!"

Paul grabbed her wrist and swung it around his neck, then rose up, adjusting her onto his back.

"Paul!"

He shambled along, carrying her piggyback. Her feet dangled

over his knees, dripping blood on his sneakers. They approached an intersection with a strip mall.

"Stop! Stop, Paul!" Cynthia slipped from his back. Holding his hand, she sat down on the curb in front of a bagel shop. Even in her altered state, she realized Paul was delusional. She needed to stall for time, calm him down. Cynthia checked her feet. The bloody grime had turned to jelly. "Let's get some water," she said.

A woman appeared beside them, and Paul spooked like a wild horse, bolting across the street. Cynthia's breath caught in her throat he slipped through the traffic, past some gas pumps, and disappeared into a convenience store.

"I said, 'Are you okay?' I'm an EMT."

Cynthia looked at the woman. Her brown hair was tied back and she wore a bumblebee pin on her summer blouse.

"Um, yeah. I'm okay."

Cynthia looked back across the street to see customers hurrying out of the minimart and then gawking through the plate-glass windows. One of them poked at his cell phone. Cynthia couldn't help thinking that it was a little bit like the Wild Safari, but now Paul was on display. The woman knelt beside Cynthia, asking her questions. Cynthia answered without really paying attention. Her attention was on the doors of the store. She hoped that Paul would stay inside until the cops came. It felt like a betrayal to wish for that, but she knew she couldn't help him. He was a danger to himself.

When the patrol car pulled into the gas station, a few of the spectators came over and talked to the cops. Cynthia stood up. "I should go over there," she said. The woman helped her hobble across the street. She watched the cops enter the store and followed behind them. Paul was asleep on the floor in front of the beer cooler. The cops tried to wake him up; then one checked his pulse. "We need an ambulance," he said to his partner, who called for one. "Hey, buddy? Can you hear me? What did you take? What are you on?"

Paul opened his eyes halfway and said, "Nothing."

Everyone from the cops at the gas station to the ambulance driver to the ER doctors asked him the same question. Even as he became less and less responsive, and his body twisted and jerked without control, his last word was "Nothing."

Cynthia stayed by his side through it all, and they always asked her next, "Come on. What did he take?"

"I don't know," Cynthia said, every time.

She couldn't rat him out to the police. But Paul's dad was on his way to the hospital, driving 150 miles because his son was in the emergency room in another state, and she knew she wouldn't be able to lie to him.

A doctor pulled the curtain aside, and Paul's dad stepped in. He was wearing jeans, a polo shirt, and a worried expression. He glanced at Cynthia then stood over Paul, who was strapped to a hospital bed, his head lolling on his neck.

"Paul, what's up? What's wrong?"

"I'm fine." His eyes didn't open.

He grabbed Paul's shoulders and brought his face closer. "You're not fine. What drugs are you on? Huh? What did you take?"

"Nothing. I'm fine."

Paul's dad turned to Cynthia. "What did he take? I know you know."

Cynthia looked past him at the doctor, then at her feet in a bucket of ice. "E."

"He took a lot of it?"

Cynthia nodded.

Paul's dad turned back to the doctor, and they discussed Paul's condition. A few hours later the three of them were driving home in the big, four-door Dodge truck. Cynthia lay across the back with her feet wrapped in ice packs. Paul sat in front, sleeping. His dad didn't say a word the whole way home.

SIX O'CLOCK: **Crisis**

Joseph Campbell writes, "[T]he cave you fear to enter holds the treasure you seek." The Crisis is the moment when the hero finally enters that cave. Although this climax usually occurs toward the end of the book or movie, it is the central crux of the narrative. Everything before this event leads up to it, and everything after this moment results from it. The Crisis is the pivotal point in the hero's journey, the instant when everything is either won or lost. It usually involves the death of the hero—whether momentary, partial, or complete—followed by his rebirth. After all, the larger plot is allegorical. Only by sacrificing himself can the hero save the world. Only by saving the world can the hero save himself.

Homer's *Odyssey* contains a powerful moment of Crisis. After a ten-year journey home, Odysseus unmasks himself in his own living room, takes up his mighty bow, and confronts the many noblemen trying to wed his wife and usurp his throne. "Dogs, did you think that I should not come back from Troy? You have wasted my substance, have forced my women servants to lie with you, and have wooed my wife while I was still living. You have feared neither god nor man, and now you shall die." Alongside his son, Telemachus, and the loyal servants of their household, Odysseus rampages against an overwhelming mob of rivals. With the help of the Olympian gods, Odysseus wins this private war, fought before his own hearth, and claims the prize he has sought for so long: the restoration of his household.

Arthurian legends offer similar dramatic turning points. After sowing discord among the Knights of the Round Table, Sir Mordred claims King Arthur's throne during his absence on campaign against Lancelot. Their two armies meet to resolve the matter through diplomacy, under strict instructions not to bare steel. But an unnamed knight is bitten by a snake and reflexively draws his sword. On that signal, the armies engage each other until a hundred thousand corpses cover the field. In the melee, King Arthur charges Mordred and runs him through with a spear but receives a mortal wound in return. In this moment of truth, Arthur saves the realm by slaying his treacherous son, but forfeits his own life.[4]

In the original *Star Wars* movie, Luke prepares to assault the Death Star, but Han Solo displays the selfishness of human nature when he refuses to join the attack. As Luke pilots his X-wing fighter into that "cave he fears to enter," Darth Vader follows him, firing his laser canons. Suddenly Han appears in the *Millennium Falcon* and eliminates Luke's pursuer. At the critical moment, Luke surrenders his dependence on technology and trusts his intuition. He makes a perfect shot, and the Death Star explodes.

Frodo Baggins faces a similar choice, holding the ring above its molten oblivion at the peak of Mount Doom. He seems as noble as Arthur, only to falter like Han Solo at the last instant. "I do not choose now to do what I came to do. I will not do this deed. The Ring is mine!"[5] Corrupted by an even greater greed, Gollum completes that final step of the quest when he accidentally falls into the volcano after biting off Frodo's ring finger. Ironically, Gollum's last act redeems him, although less intentionally than Han Solo's change of heart.

Today's heroine, Katniss Everdeen, culminates the Hunger Games by joining Peeta Mellark in a double suicide threat, simultaneously overcoming her distrust of others and her fear of dominion by the all-powerful rulers of Panem. Her bluff works, and the gamemasters back down, granting her and Peeta a joint victory.

• • •

When Colin finally gets his day in court, he feels every step has led toward this day. The nameless shadow of an absent father has trailed behind him since birth—to Little League sign-ups, to birthday parties, to every class in school. Colin expects the actual man to celebrate their relationship or at least say hello. Instead, Tim rejects his son, deflecting Colin's journey down a different road.

Cynthia has ridden a roller coaster over the past year, speeding through the whiplash turns and loops of her relationship with Paul, riding the unpredictable rails of different drugs. In the most reckless free fall of their misadventures, they wind up in a hospital emergency room, lucky to escape with their lives. It's a pattern that is bound to continue, as a roller coaster climbs its trembling scaffold for another terrifying lap. With her slashed and bloody feet, Cynthia decides that she's getting off this ride.

Reflecting on your past, can you relate to Cynthia's experience? Have you ever been trapped in a pattern that you finally broke free of? Maybe you were stuck in a lousy job, or hooked on cigarettes, or going in circles within a relationship. Looking back, what was the moment of Crisis that made it possible for you to identify and break that cycle?

Perhaps you've had an experience closer to Colin's, a long journey that climbed doggedly up a steep slope to the summit. At the end of that difficult path, you finally faced your greatest fear, and it changed your life. What was that moment?

Look into the faces of your teens. What are they afraid of? Ridicule? Failure? Growing up? Whatever each teen's personal dragon, her road of trials will ultimately lead to that cave she fears to enter, where her old life will be burned away. Hopefully she will slay her metaphorical nemesis in the process. Either way, she will emerge transformed. When the outcome isn't as glamorous as our fictional models, it can seem like the end of the world. In a way, it is. But in every crisis lies opportunity, and in every pivot point, the chance for a new direction.

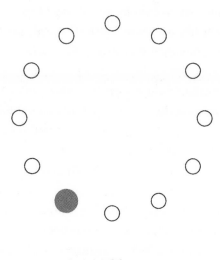

CHAPTER 7

Treasure

S ix o'clock changed everything, and the hero is rewarded. The wicked witch melts away, and Dorothy gains the magic slippers. The Athenians are safe now that Theseus has slain the Minotaur. Odin survives his ordeal on the World Tree, winning the runes and increasing his power.

SEVEN O'CLOCK: **Colin Set Free**

Colin stood in front of Papi's Deli with Alicia and Mary Ann waiting for the bus on his first day of middle school. The fecund heat of summer still hung over the nearby reservoir, redolent with summer laziness. Alicia was wearing designer shorts and a trendy polo shirt; Mary Ann was checking her fingernails. Colin adjusted his baggy khaki shorts, slung low below his T-shirt. His sneakers were brand-new but not top-of-the-line Nikes.

The bus rolled to a stop, and Colin let the girls on first. He followed them down the aisle, but when Alicia and Mary Ann sat near the middle, Colin continued to the back of the bus—a seventh grader staking his claim in eighth-grade territory. This was the second stop, so there was only one older student already there. He and Amet knew that if they could claim a backseat on the first day, they would own it all year.

They'd been riding the bus together since third grade. After school they rode bikes to each other's houses to play football in Colin's backyard or basketball in Amet's driveway. Amet's mom used to think Colin was a bad kid because he had long hair, but then she got to know him. The bus drivers got to know them over those four years too. They were always up to something.

The bus stopped and Amet led a crowd on board. He wore khakis and a plaid, short-sleeved, button-down shirt. He was the only Indian kid in school, except for Sanjay. Amet sat down next to Colin and pulled something out of his pants pocket. He held it in his open hand beside his hip so that only Colin could see it.

"Check this out," he said.

It was a glass vial about the size of a cigarette lighter.

"What is it?" Colin said.

"It's a stink bomb. It works like a glow stick. You smash it, and the two liquids mix together. It makes a huge stink."

Colin looked more closely and saw the outline of a smaller, yellow cylinder floating inside it. The bus stopped. Matt and a few more kids got on.

"Do it!" Colin said.

"No way. Not on the bus."

"Why not?"

"I don't know."

"I'll do it." Colin said.

"Seriously?"

Colin checked the wide mirror above the driver. The old woman was focused on the road. She slowed and stopped for another crowd of students. "Yeah. Why not? Give it to me." He opened his hand, and Amet slid the warm ampoule into Colin's palm. Colin figured the liquid would leave an incriminating puddle, and he didn't want that to be directly under his seat, so he stretched his leg into the aisle and struck up a conversation with Matt in the opposite seat. "Hey, dude. Ready for the first day of school, or what?" He didn't really listen to the answer. Resting his elbow on his knee, he dropped the stink bomb on the floor beside his foot and stomped it under his heel.

The effect was instantaneous. The bus was a hot dumpster of rotten eggs. Colin covered his mouth and threw himself against Amet, whose head was already out a window, along with everybody else's. Everyone was shouting, retching, and scrambling for fresh air. The driver pulled the bus to the roadside.

"Alright, who did it?" she said. She was old, wrinkled, and bent. "We're not moving until we find out who did it." The bus was full of unfamiliar kids on the first day of the year. She didn't know who to accuse.

Colin and Amet looked at each other and gasped for air at an open window like everybody else. As the bus driver marched up and down the aisle haranguing the students, the odor slowly dissipated.

"Was it you? Was it you?" She pointed randomly.

Nobody answered, so she eventually started the bus and continued to school.

• • •

As they filed off the bus, Colin and Amet smiled politely and wished the driver good morning. Once inside the middle school building, they relived the event in whispers on the way to Earth Science, their first class of the year. The room had rows of counter-high lab tables, each with a small sink and Bunsen burner. Colin and Amet took the table in the back, swallowing their laughter.

The bell rang, and the teacher began. "Good morning, and welcome to honors Earth Science. My name is Mr. Borstensen. The first thing we're going to do is discuss the safety protocols for lab. I'm passing out the information you'll need—" He was interrupted by an announcement over the intercom.

"Colin McIntyre, please report to the principal's office. Colin McIntyre, you're needed in the main office. Thank you."

Colin stopped breathing, the skin on his neck seemed to shrink, and his bladder threatened to spill. Mr. B slid one finger down his attendance book and looked from boy to boy. Their eyes met. "Colin?"

"Yup." Colin said.

"You'll have to get the notes from a friend."

• • •

The principal, Mr. Gandalfini, sat behind his imposing desk, cluttered with trays of papers, his brass nameplate, a mug of pens, and a snow globe. "Well, the first class on the first day of school, and you're already in the principal's office. How about that?"

Colin tried to look baffled and angelic.

"What happened on the bus this morning?"

"The bus driver pulled over."

"That's what I heard. Why did she pull over?"

"There was a horrible smell."

"Who was responsible for that?"

"I don't know. I thought maybe we drove past a skunk or something."

"You don't think the smell was coming from inside the bus?"

"It could have, I guess."

"But you don't know anything about it."

"No."

Mr. Gandalfini looked at Colin for a long minute. "Okay. Thanks. You can go back to class."

• • •

Every kid on the bus was called down, individually, and word got around that some of them had talked. At least Jeremy had the stones to admit it at lunch. "They told me they already knew who it was, but they were giving every kid the same chance to come clean and not get detention. So I told. I didn't want to get detention! And besides, they said they already knew." Colin was called to the office again after lunch.

Mr. Gandalfini didn't mince words. "Colin, we've talked to everyone who was on the bus this morning, and it's become clear that you were responsible for the stink bomb. You'll serve one day of in-school suspension as a consequence. This is middle school, not elementary school, and you need to use better judgment. Is that clear?"

"How can you give me suspension? What's your proof?"

"We have witnesses."

"Who?"

"I don't need to tell you that."

"Those kids could be lying because *they* did it. They *say* I did it; I *say* I didn't. Why do you believe *them* and not *me*?"

"We have multiple witnesses."

"Who? I want to know. I'll bet they did it. You can't suspend me without proof."

"You'll report to in-school suspension on Friday morning. You'll have time to do your classwork and to think about your actions. Colin, I hope this is the last time we have this kind of conversation, but that's up to you."

Colin left the office in a cloud of middle-school glory and half-hearted outrage. He felt wronged by a totalitarian system of justice based on secret testimony and zero physical evidence, even if he was guilty! On the other hand, now that he was busted, he might as well enjoy the fame. The whole school had already heard the story of "the stink bomb on the bus." Soon they would all know the daredevil who had pulled that stunt: Colin McIntyre.

Hopefully his mom wouldn't find out.

● ● ●

Kelly reacted to the news with exasperation, then relief. She had been watching her son closely since that day at the courthouse when his biological father had literally turned his back on Colin. He didn't cry, but when that courthouse door closed, so did something inside Colin. That shrine in his heart went dark. He walked out to the car with his mom and his aunt, and they drove him home, wondering how he could be so calm.

That summer, Colin played manhunt and backyard football with the neighborhood kids just like always, or rode his bike to play basketball with Amet. Kelly talked with Colin about Tim, probing for repressed anger but finding none. She kept waiting for the other shoe to drop, for the shock wave of that rejection bombshell to finally arrive and flatten him. It never did. In Colin's mind, the case was closed. The Super Dad of his imagination didn't exist, and his actual, biological father was a jerk. Colin was matter-of-fact. "Mom, I'm not missing out on *him*; he's missing out on *me*." The same indomitable mind-set that ruffled teachers' feathers allowed Colin to dismiss Tim from his mind.

The stink bomb prank would be "acting out" for a quiet kid, but it was reassuringly standard behavior for Colin, who continued to find himself in hot water that fall, especially with Mr. Borstensen. Once, Colin left Home Economics class with a new laundry bag he'd just stitched together. Amet climbed inside it, and Colin dragged him across the waxed floor of the crowded hallway, toppling kids like bowling pins. The hundred-pound, bright yellow sack caused chaos for a few minutes; then Colin and Amet raced to Study Hall. Mr. Borstensen happened to be the study hall proctor that period. He overheard them celebrating the stunt and sent them to the principal's office. Detention, again.

But Colin's impulsive behavior didn't undercut his academic performance. On his first-quarter report card, all of his grades were above 85, and he scored perfect 100s in Algebra and Earth Science. Meanwhile, Kelly finished her teaching degree at Mount St. Mary College and got her first teaching job as a home instructor for kids unable to attend school. One of her students was laid up after a kidney transplant; another had bone disease. She had six students altogether, forty hours total, and she still cleaned houses on the side. Over the winter, Tim's court-ordered weekly child-support payment of fifty-nine dollars stopped arriving in her mailbox. Kelly made a few calls and learned that Tim had skipped town, abandoning his wife and children.

As time stretched on with no news, Colin joked about leading a posse of his friends to track Tim down and serve him with legal papers. He fantasized about recovering a windfall of overdue child support and going on a shopping spree. Eventually this amusement grew stale and faded, along with any thought of Tim. Eliminating the paternal mystery had resolved the blank space in Colin's understanding of his origins, but he still yearned for the material benefits of a dual-income household.

Colin celebrated his fourteenth birthday with a trip to the Orange County Government Center in Goshen. Kelly drove their ramshackle Honda up Route 17, and Colin had all his documentation in a manila envelope on his lap: the signed application form, a note from his middle school guidance office, the results of a physical exam, and a notarized copy of his birth certificate. When they returned home an hour later, he held his blue New York State "permission to work" card.

As soon as they got inside the house, Colin opened the *Times-Herald Record* to the classifieds. "Go for it, buddy. Let me know if you need any help." Kelly went to her room to prepare lessons for her home-instruction students. Colin scanned the telephone numbers in the newspaper ads. Most of his friends' numbers started with the same three digits, all within biking distance. He noticed one ad for a busboy and called out from the kitchen, "Mom, where's 351?"

"Tuxedo."

A few kids on Colin's bus route lived in Tuxedo, right up the hill. He dialed the number.

● ● ●

Later that week, Colin's Aunt Lee drove him to the address he'd written in the margin of the newspaper page. He wore his chorus outfit: white shirt and black pants.

"You're going to be great, Colin," Aunt Lee said, turning off Benjamin Meadow Road onto Route 201.

"Yeah, I know."

"Let's do a little role play to get you warmed up." She affected a male voice. "What makes you think you'd be good at this job?"

"Well, I'm pretty strong, and I work hard."

Aunt Lee suppressed a laugh. "Can you give me an example of a time in the past when you worked hard?"

"Um . . . hmm. Yeah."

"If you need time to think, that's fine, but say something like, 'I'm glad you asked,' or 'That's an excellent question.' It's polite, and it gives you a chance to put your thoughts in order."

"I'm glad you asked. When our church's youth group had a car wash, I worked all day. I washed the first car and the last car, and I helped clean up. We made $647 for our trip to Six Flags."

"Nice one!" Aunt Lee coached him through some more stock interview questions, then turned off onto Tuxedo Road. She stopped at a security gate. A picturesque guard booth with cedar shingles split the two lanes. Fourteen-foot fieldstone walls stretched into the woods in both directions.

"May I help you?" the Tuxedo Park police officer asked, leaning out the top half of a Dutch door.

"We're looking for the restaurant . . . for a job interview?"

"Name please?"

"Colin McIntyre."

The officer checked a clipboard and then looked up. "Straight up the hill to the top. Follow signs for parking." The gate rose in salute. They glided up the wooded road past secluded driveways to the country club and parked beside Jaguars and BMWs. Inside, the receptionist introduced them to a tall woman in a pantsuit.

"Good afternoon. I'm Marge Jocey, assistant general manager."

"LeeAnn McIntyre. Nice to meet you."

"Pleased to meet you. I'm Colin McIntyre."

"Why don't the two of us go into the dining room and have a chat?"

"Yes, ma'am."

Ms. Jocey led the way, glancing at her watch. She stopped beside a round table overlooking the lake and gestured to a chair.

"Thank you." Colin said, and they sat down simultaneously.

"What have you got there?" she asked.

Colin opened his file folder and slid his blue working papers across the white tablecloth. "These are my working papers because I'm fourteen."

"You came prepared. So, Colin, tell me why you want to work as a busboy here at the Tuxedo Club."

"I want to save up money for college and for a car."

"Big plans, and you raise the question of transportation. How would you get to work without a car?"

"My mom said she would drive me."

"I see. Do you mind if I ask a few other questions?"

"Go right ahead."

"What would you say is your greatest weakness?"

"I'm glad you asked. I'd have to say that my greatest weakness is that I'm a perfectionist. I want to make sure that I do things the right way, and sometimes that takes a little extra time."

A pause.

"Good answer." Ms. Jocey leaned closer. "Would you say that you're a follower or a leader?"

"That's a great question. I'd say that I'm a follower *and* a leader. I always follow instructions, but I also think for myself and propose new ideas."

"Is that right?" Ms. Jocey tried to hide a smile.

●   ●   ●

Colin reported for work the following weekend, joining a crew of middle-aged Mexican men who taught him how to clear and set tables. He soon learned that nineteenth-century titans of industry had founded the club and the whole village of Tuxedo Park as a weekend retreat. One of them had introduced the short dinner jacket as a replacement for the more formal black tailcoat. The fashion caught on, and the name "tuxedo" stuck. Now the private lake was rimmed with mansions, and exotic cars flashed along the winding narrow roads.

When Colin got his first paycheck two weeks later, he opened it as Kelly drove him home.

"How much?" she asked.

"$147.67."

"Nice job! What are you going to do with it, Mr. Moneybags?"

"I'm thinking about getting my own apartment."

Kelly laughed, "Well, don't forget about utilities and food."

"They feed us at work. And I'd have dinner with you on my days off."

"Good plan. And how will you get to work? You could lease a Porsche."

"Don't be silly, Mom. I don't have my license yet, so a taxi of course."

"Of course."

* * *

Colin worked every weekend at the club through the last months of school. He was the only busboy who spoke English, so he handled lots of special requests—gluten free or extra horseradish. The members took a shine to this plucky, resourceful youngster and tipped him generously. Colin started to think of himself as one of them, as an inevitable member of their club and future Lamborghini owner. His grades rose with his self-esteem, and the year ended with New York State Regents exams in the gym.

The Earth Science exam was after lunch, and Colin was nervous about seeing Mr. Borstensen again. At the middle-school dance three nights earlier, Colin had been swaying with a classmate named Danielle when he found himself locked in the first real kiss of his life. In the crowded, dimly lit gym, they tested the thrilling limits of their innocence, their lips fumbling and unfamiliar—until Mr. Borstensen yanked Colin by the shoulder and parked him against the wall. "Stay here until the song is over," he said and then turned to scan the room for more smooching couples. During the last chorus, Colin slipped away into the shadows and hid from Mr. B until the dance ended.

Today Colin entered the same gymnasium, now brightly lit and filled by a sea of tiny desktops, arranged in uniform rows over both basketball courts. Colin found a seat and waited for the clock to strike. Mr. Borstensen didn't mention the dance when he handed Colin a sealed test booklet, nor when Colin turned in his answers first, as usual. When his report card came in the mail a few weeks later, Colin had the last laugh. Straight As for the year, and 100 percent on the Honors Earth Science final exam.

SEVEN O'CLOCK: **Cynthia Hangs On**

Cynthia sat on Paul's bed, waiting for him to text her again. The tension in the house had been building ever since the debacle at Six Flags two weeks ago. Driving back from New Jersey in the dark that night, nobody had said a word. Every day since, Paul and his dad had kept opposite schedules, business as usual. They were never in the same room together, but the unspoken accusations and rebuttals hung in the air like vapor awaiting a spark. And Paul had decided to confront his dad today after work.

Cynthia couldn't shake the feeling that everything was about to come crashing down. They had pushed their luck too far. The cops would catch up to them, and they would go to jail. Or Paul would overdose again, and it would be fatal. To dodge such a fate, Cynthia had quit dealing completely and stopped using drugs. She'd even started seeing a therapist and wanted Paul to see one too. He wanted to handle things himself.

She heard Paul come in the front door and thump up the stairs. As soon as he opened the bedroom door, she noticed that his pupils were overlarge.

"Are you alright?" she said.

"Yeah." Paul's polo shirt and basketball shorts hung from his lean frame, and his eyes were wide and intense.

"How much . . . how hard are you tripping?"

Cynthia knew Paul had prepared for the conversation with his dad. He had an eyedropper bottle that contained a residue of LSD and brought it to work with him. He filled it with grain alcohol that morning, shook it, then poured the solution under his tongue. He held it there for a minute before spitting it out. He did that three times. By the time he finished work that afternoon, he was peaking.

"I'm gonna talk to him now."

Cynthia had been trying to talk him out of this idea all week. He wanted to talk to his dad about his drug use, but he needed to be high during that conversation? It was absurd and ironic. Ultimately Paul wanted to transfer to the main UConn campus in Storrs, two hours away, instead of commuting to the Waterbury campus. Cynthia could see this was a stupid idea. He planned to move in with his friend Zach, who was a total drug fiend. Plus, Storrs was a lot harder academically. Paul dismissed her objections.

Cynthia stood up and followed Paul downstairs to the living room, which had tall, Victorian windows. High school graduation portraits and family photos hung on azure walls. Paul's dad was lying on the sofa in sweatpants and a T-shirt, watching TV. He'd gone to work at the factory at four in the morning, as usual, and he was dozing before dinner. He always complained about the couch's broken springs, but he slept there anyway.

Cynthia sat down on the loveseat, and Paul stood beside her. "Dad, I need to talk to you about something."

Paul's dad muted the big-screen television. He was smaller than Paul, and his black hair was starting to gray. He had the weather-beaten face of a reformed alcoholic. His tired eyes met Paul's, and he paused. Then he pressed the power button on the remote and sat up.

Paul spoke, and the words came out in torrent. "I need to talk to you because I don't want to go to Waterbury anymore. I want to go to Storrs. I've been thinking about it for a while, and that's where I want to go. I'm not happy here. I need a change. I need to get out on my own. I don't like my job. I used to like it, but now I don't. They drink there. Every day. I drink too. I know it's stupid, but I have to because I hate it so much, so I have to get drunk just to be there. And that's part of why I hate it."

He was pacing, clipping the coffee table with his shins at each turn.

"And I don't want to let you down. I know I'm letting you down, and I don't want to. I know I let you down at Six Flags, and I hate myself for it. I was so messed up. But it wasn't just Ecstasy. We did acid too. We deal acid, Dad. And Ecstasy. And pills. Cynthia gets them from work."

Cynthia froze. *Where was he going with this?*

"We buy the acid in Massachusetts. Then we sell it down here. We make money, Dad. A lot of money. And I can't stop. I have the car bill and tuition bills. I can't stop. And Tom deals too. He deals everything with all his druggie friends. It's all around me. I can't get away from it! And he's collecting unemployment. Even while he's working. And when he's coming down too hard, he calls out sick to work. He told them Mom was in the hospital. Then he told them Mom died. He's a total fuck-up."

He wasn't shouting, but his voice was louder than normal.

"And you and Mom put all this pressure on me. I'm stressed out all the time trying not to mess up like him, and I just can't take it anymore. That's why I want to go to Storrs. I can start over and get cleaned up. It will be a better place for me. I'm just so stressed out here. I just need to get out."

He went on like that for a long time, saying the same things in different ways.

"Okay. I understand," his dad said, interrupting him. "Why didn't you tell me any of this?"

"I'm not complaining. I know I need to work and go to school. I just want to do it where I want to do it. I talked to UConn, and they'll let me transfer if you sign the papers, and then I can sign up for classes at Storrs." Paul had tears in his eyes.

Paul's dad stood up. "I'll sign. Of course I'll sign. If that's what you think will help you, Paul. It's going to be okay. You're going to be okay." He gripped Paul's arms. They embraced. Cynthia watched them from the loveseat, seeing clearly that Paul had conned his dad into believing this was a good thing, that this would change his behavior. Paul even believed it himself, but Cynthia finally knew better. The only thing that would change was his address. All at once, Cynthia remembered the day they went skydiving together. Only now she was still on the plane, watching Paul free-fall.

SEVEN O'CLOCK: **Treasure**

In the monomyth cycle, the hero who survives his or her greatest ordeal gains some reward or treasure. Frodo regains his self-control after ridding himself of the One Ring. Luke Skywalker and the

Rebel Alliance secure their liberation from the Empire as the Death Star explodes. Odysseus reclaims his home through a bloody victory within its very walls. Katniss Everdeen wins her own life and Peeta's by defying the gamemasters. The Treasure can be material, emotional, or both. Every time James Bond thwarts his enemy, innocent lives are spared, but 007 also gains personal satisfaction from outwitting an evil mastermind.

Paul's Six Flags overdose brought him to a crisis that he and Cynthia had so far managed to avoid. At the end of the line, Paul lied to the police, doctors, and nurses who tried to help them. He even lied to his own father. Cynthia stayed true to Paul in spite of her better judgment, only veering toward honesty when Paul's dad asked her directly. At that moment, she began to peel away from Paul, charting a separate course.

Colin's biological father rejected him without a glance. Colin did not win the prize he had anticipated—a loving, involved father— but he did reap some treasure in his quest for resolution. Certainty replaced uncertainty. A constellation of possibilities spiraled away, dissolving his hopes but leaving a stone-hard kernel of undisputed truth. Colin didn't waste another minute pining for that man in the courthouse. Instead he came to his own rescue.

Cynthia's ordeal was self-inflicted. She mixed three illegal drugs, and only the dumb luck of her body chemistry spared her from Paul's fate, or worse. Paul missed the whole lesson, unconscious during the worst of his ordeal, unreflective after he awoke. But Cynthia saw his dad's face at the hospital and again in the living room, tortured by his reckless son's thoughtless decisions. He loved Paul so much, but Paul didn't spare a thought for anyone else. Watching it play out between them, Cynthia recognized the dynamic, like looking through a shop window at someone who's standing just like you, then realizing it's your own reflection in the glass. That realization was her Treasure, a gut-level awareness of her own self-destructive momentum.

Colin and Cynthia both emerge from their Crises with Treasures, but not the ones they were expecting. There is a similar twist in *The Wonderful Wizard of Oz*. Dorothy and her friends defeat the Wicked

Witch of the West, and the Wizard grants them all prizes, but these are simply tokens of the Treasures they have already gained through their heroic deeds. The Scarecrow always wanted a brain, so the Wizard gives him a diploma, merely recognizing the intelligence he has displayed throughout the quest. The Tin Woodman is delighted when the Wizard gives him a velvet heart stuffed with sawdust, yet he was always compassionate and emotional during their travails. Likewise, the Cowardly Lion always performed courageous deeds, even before the Wizard gives him a dish of liquid that alleviates his self-consciousness. Dorothy is made aware that she can return home by means of the ruby slippers that she has been wearing all along. All four of them possessed these Treasures the whole time.

Odysseus vanquishes his rivals in the great hall, risking his own life, his son's, and the legacy of his ancestors. He declares himself to Penelope, his loyal wife, who had sustained his household and her fidelity for the past ten, long years. She doesn't recognize him and demands that he prove his identity. During her speech, she instructs her maids to dismantle her marriage bed and reassemble it in the hall. Odysseus is shocked—he built the bed himself in such a way that it could not be moved. Penelope recognizes the dismay in his face, betraying his knowledge of that intimate nuptial secret. Odysseus wins her heart anew, the greatest Treasure of his life: eternally faithful Penelope.

In *Star Wars*, Luke destroys the Death Star. At that climactic moment, he relinquishes his dependence on technology, allowing the Force to guide his actions. In the same moment, Han Solo transcends his selfishness in a dangerous, altruistic gambit. Both heroes seal the victory by overcoming their personal insecurities, emancipating the innocent victims of the evil Empire in the process.

Fictional heroes triumph over impossible odds to win enormous stakes, and those moments are climactic and satisfying. After the dust settles, the hero often recognizes unexpected elements in the reward, which twist the story around another turn. Likewise, teenagers in the real world are often surprised by the emotional or material consequences of their actions, even though adult observers might have seen what was coming—and given them plenty of warnings! Sifting through the rubble afterward, what is most essential remains intact but has been transformed. For teenagers who secure a spot on the starting team, earn a pivotal grade, or win the heart of a paramour, that victory might be supremely fulfilling, or it might feel unexpectedly hollow.

Can you remember the aftermath of a turning point in your life? Did it play out as expected or take you by surprise? What about your teens? They might need your help understanding the Treasure they've uncovered.

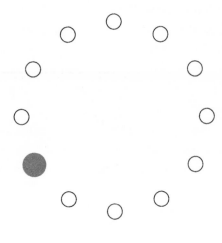

CHAPTER 8

Result

The eighth hour describes the aftermath of the hero's pivotal victory. Zeus retaliates with Pandora's box after Prometheus steals fire from the gods. Katniss Everdeen is subtly accused of sedition following the Hunger Games. Flying eagles rescue Frodo after he destroys the One Ring. Odysseus awaits retaliation by the families of those he has slain.

EIGHT O'CLOCK: **Colin Tests the Limit**

Kids in the basic math classes thought Mr. Harris was great because he made stupid jokes and laughed at himself, but Colin's honors level classmates knew he was a terrible teacher. As he drew a triangle inside a circle on the blackboard, he started to explain the formulas for calculating the areas of various spaces in the diagram.

"That's wrong." Colin said.

"Excuse me? Colin, do you have a question?"

"No, I just want to point out that the formula you just wrote down on the board is wrong."

"Oh, really?" Mr. Harris looked at it and quickly erased it. "Well, perhaps you'd like to write the correct one?" He held out the chalk to Colin.

"Sure." Colin stood up and took the chalk from his teacher's hand. "So, first we need to calculate the area of the circle. That's two times pi times the radius, squared. Then we need to calculate the area of the triangle, which is one-half the base times the height. We subtract the area of the triangle from the area of the circle, and that gives us the total area of these three shaded sections." Colin put the chalk down and walked toward his desk.

"Where are you going?"

Colin stopped. "To my seat."

"But you're not finished yet. What about a rhomboid inside a circle?"

"Sure, that's easy." Colin drew another circle on the board and carefully inscribed a four-sided figure just like the diagram in their Geometry book. He knew Mr. Harris was waiting for him to make a mistake. Colin explained the formulas for area as he had before. "Any questions?" His eyes swept the room and then rested on Mr. Harris.

"Yes, actually. How can you calculate the angles of the rhomboid?"

"Well, we know that the sum of the angles of any quadrilateral must equal 360. If these two sides are similar," Colin marked the sides with chalk, "and these two sides are similar, then the rhomboid is symmetrical, so these two angles will be similar, and so will these two."

Colin had learned some geometry in Math Club last year, and he'd already read the whole chapter last night, because he knew Mr. Harris would do a terrible job of teaching it. The bell rang; Mr. Harris announced the homework assignment, and everyone rushed out the door except Colin, who walked out slowly without saying a word.

Colin's in-your-face approach to learning didn't always work out so well. Teachers sometimes kicked him out of classes for his outbursts, and his honors English teacher even demoted him to the standard English class. Such encounters only convinced Colin that teachers weren't interested in promoting actual learning. They just wanted to catch you making a mistake; the teacher-student relationship was a petty contest of wills.

His attitude changed on the first day of Trigonometry class in tenth grade. His new teacher, Mr. Hodges, wore a black suit, white shirt, and designer necktie. All the other teachers in school just wore a polo shirt and khakis.

Halfway through calling roll, he read aloud, "Colin McIntyre."

"Present." Colin said. There was a pause. Colin saw a flash of recognition in his teacher's face, and he knew his unruly reputation had preceded him.

"Do you have any family in Pine Bush?" Mr. Hodges asked.

The question caught Colin off guard. "Yeah, my mom grew up there, and my uncle teaches at the middle school."

"Any relation to Mr. Mac, who taught English at Pine Bush High?"

"He was my grandfather." Colin sat up a little straighter.

"Miiista McIntyre, your grandfather was the best teacher I ever had, and I *hated* English." He nodded and then continued down the list of names.

Colin didn't speak out of turn that day in Trig, or that week. He raised his hand before calling out his answers. Mr. Hodges used the first names of his other students, but always called Colin by the name of his favorite teacher, "Mr. Mac." Colin's voice rang out in response, but without the bluster it carried in his other classes.

Mr. Hodges taught with passion and high energy. He brought the formulas to life with stories of Descartes and Euclid. He called out pop questions, acronyms, and mnemonic devices while working through a problem on the board, encouraging wrong answers and student-led problem solving. When Colin blurted out some tangential remark, Mr. Hodges laughed and redirected him instead of shutting him down. Those forty-five minutes passed too quickly every day, and Colin woke up each morning looking forward to them.

As the president of the teacher's union, Mr. Hodges sometimes attended meetings with the school board during business hours, and his substitute teachers didn't appreciate Colin's overeager class participation. In fact, every time there was a Trig substitute, Colin wound up standing in the hall until the final bell. He knew the drill from his other classes. When Mr. Hodges returned the following day, he always read the substitute's report and scolded the class for misbehaving, singling out his prize student, Mr. Mac. But his rebukes were halfhearted. The day before his next absence, he reminded the class to behave for the substitute, and the day after, he started class with the same opening line. "How was class yesterday? Let me guess. You guys tortured the substitute teacher and Mr. Mac got kicked out. Am I right?" He was always right.

When Colin's mom came in for parent conferences, she heard the usual reports of Colin's disruptive behavior and untapped potential from his other teachers, but Mr. Hodges assured her that Colin's gears simply spun faster than the high school's. "All these rules are keeping him boxed in. As soon as he gets out of high school, he'll take off."

In eleventh grade, Colin signed up for Calculus and Statistics, both taught by Mr. Hodges. While he completed a homework assignment at the kitchen table one night, his mom sorted through the day's mail and handed him a pamphlet. "You keep talking about how much you love your math classes. Maybe you should do this." Colin read about Clarkson University's program for outstanding math and science students who wanted to skip twelfth grade and go straight to college. It seemed ideal: Escape the prison of high school, fast-forward to independence, and study nothing but math.

"Mom, I want to do this."

"Well, go online and see what's involved. Let me know how I can help, but I'm not going to push you."

Colin studied the website and downloaded the application forms. He needed to submit his grades, SAT scores, a personal essay, and three letters of recommendation. Colin knew he could count on Mr. Hodges for one of them, but he wasn't sure whom to ask for the other two. His other teachers couldn't stand him. Colin still worked at the Tuxedo Club on weekends, and he thought about asking his boss to write him a letter. In the Golf House dining room one Saturday, he was setting out glasses, still hot from the dishwasher, when a club member approached him.

"Hey, Colin. What's new?" Mr. Palumbo ran an underwater construction company that handled huge projects like bridges and dams. He always went out of his way to talk to Colin. They talked about Colin's math classes, about the car he hoped to buy from his aunt. Then Colin realized that a letter from the head of a successful engineering firm would look great on his application.

"Actually, can I ask you a favor?"

"Sure, what is it?" Mr. Palumbo said.

"I'm applying to Clarkson University. If I get in, I can study engineering there next year. Do you think you could write a letter of recommendation for me?"

"Clarkson University? Actually, I play golf with a couple of guys who went to Clarkson. I think I can get you two letters of recommendation. From alumni."

"Thanks!" Colin shook his hand and watched him walk out to meet his foursome. The fantasy described on that brochure moved a step closer to reality.

Mr. Palumbo's plan bore fruit, and Colin slowly assembled all the admission requirements, but he wasn't watching the calendar. With the application deadline looming, Colin's mom woke him up early one Saturday morning. "Colin, wake up. There's an SAT at the high school today. You can pay the late registration fee and take the test today. It's your last chance if you want Clarkson to get your scores in time."

Colin rolled out of bed, grabbed his calculator, and drove to school. The testing room was almost empty, since it was so late in the college application cycle. All the other students were seniors, probably making a third or fourth reach for that elusive higher score. Colin whipped through the math section, familiar with all the material from his classes with Mr. Hodges. When he got to a question about cross-multiplying polynomials, "DUPA!" echoed in his head. His whole class cried out as one whenever Mr. Hodges solved a problem on the board, reminding them "Down, UP, and Across spells? DUPA!" When he handed over his test with Clarkson listed to receive his scores, he felt invincible. How could he not get accepted?

●   ●   ●

When Colin got home from school one day in March, Kelly showed him an envelope with Clarkson College's green-and-white logo in the return address.

"Cool," he said and walked past her.

"Aren't you going to read it?" Kelly asked.

"I know I got in," Colin said, opening the fridge. With letters from two Clarkson alumni and a math SAT score of 790 out of 800, he had no doubt.

"You're so obnoxious." Kelly carefully levered open the flap and unfolded the paper inside. "We are pleased to inform you . . ."

"Told you." Colin took a gulp of milk from the bottle. He felt no shock at the news, but he did feel a thrill of victory. The long battle of high school was decided, and he'd won. Colin still went to class every day and earned decent grades, but the anxiety was gone. He had nothing to prove anymore. He was a free man.

Colin's outgoing personality had always shielded his uncertainty, but that vulnerable center solidified into self-confidence with his Clarkson acceptance. All those negative teachers who had tried to keep him down with punishments and demotions were full of shit. They had underestimated him. He was going to college a year early because of his smarts. But for all his newfound conviction, Colin still had trouble talking to girls. He was about to finish high school, and he'd never even had a girlfriend. That kiss on the dance floor and a few pecks at summer camp were the sum of his love life.

During the last month of school, Colin started going to the weekend parties, something he'd never done before. He was popular enough, even elected class president in ninth grade, but he avoided parties because he didn't drink alcohol, and that's what high school parties were all about. After watching his mother attending AA meetings all his life and seeing his grandfather waste away, Colin knew what could happen and was paranoid about getting hooked.

But his sense of liberation needed release, so he drove his friends to the parties but didn't drink himself. When they offered him beer or liquor, he flew his nonconformist flag. "I'll never drink that stuff. It tastes nasty!" While his friends raced through cups of beer and did keg stands, Colin grabbed a two-liter bottle of Sprite and chugged it down in one go. This satirical stunt became his signature feat at every party that spring.

As the school year wound down, he cruised through exam week, attending a different party at a different house each night. Finally, on the eve of his last exam, he decided to drink a beer. Students crowded around the silver keg in its red plastic tub filled with ice. Colin held a two-liter bottle of soda over his head, and everyone cheered to see his trick. This time, his impulsive spirit pushed through a new boundary. He handed Amet the bottle in exchange for his beer. The crowd roared and raised their cups to him. Colin swallowed the foamy liquid and held the cup high, upside-down to prove it empty. More cheers.

Colin didn't stop at one drink. He finally joined his classmates in their dizzy state of euphoria. As the night wore on, he slipped deeper and deeper under its spell. He found himself chatting with a girl from his English class at one point. She was laughing at something he said. Colin kept the conversation going while simultaneously thinking about how wonderful it was to flirt with a girl. Matt interrupted him to say it was time to head home.

"Are you coming?"

"No, I'll get a ride." Colin said, slurring his words.

"Dude, don't forget; you're picking me up tomorrow at 8:30, right? The AP Physics exam."

"See you tomorrow." Colin said.

"My house; 8:30," Matt said.

Colin winked. "I got you."

● ● ●

Colin opened his eyes. He was lying in his bed at home, still wearing his clothes from the night before, and Matt was shaking him awake. His eyeballs throbbed in his head.

"Dude! Wake up!"

"What time is it?"

"The test starts in five minutes! Come on! My dad's waiting outside!"

Colin stumbled out of bed and followed Matt through the screen door into the pulverizing June sunlight. He slid carefully into the backseat and gently closed the car door. Matt slammed his, and the car backed up.

"I'm sorry, man," Colin said. The headache pounded behind his eyes, and the moving car made him queasy.

"I've been calling you for an hour. My dad came home from work to get me. I made him stop here in case you were in a coma or something."

"I'm sorry, Mr. C."

"Well, let's just hope you two didn't study a year of Physics only to lose four AP credits by missing the exam. And by the way, you smell terrible."

"Yeah, you smell like barf, dude."

Colin looked at the stain on his jeans. "I'm sorry."

●　●　●

Colin and Matt walked into the school gymnasium, a silent matrix of desk chairs and scribbling students. A teacher rushed over to them, checked their IDs, and led them to empty seats. She handed them their sealed exam packets and gave them instructions. "The exam period runs from nine o'clock to eleven o'clock." She emphasized the nine.

Colin got to work, but his eyeballs hurt every time they jumped from test booklet to answer sheet. His thoughts were slow and sticky, and his stomach rolled. His mouth tasted like burnt socks. These physics questions seemed much harder than the ones they'd practiced in class, and Colin had to unpack each sentence to make sure he understood it. He drew diagrams and worked out equations in his little blue book while proctors circulated among the desks. Colin stopped writing when he noticed a pair of black leather shoes and dark trousers beside him. He looked up into the face of Mr. Hodges, his favorite math teacher.

"Mr. Mac, are you drunk?"

Colin tried to read Mr. Hodges' expression. He'd been so proud of Colin's SAT score and Clarkson acceptance, and now he was seeing his star pupil at his worst, smelling like a subway bum. Colin knew he risked getting kicked out of the exam, but he couldn't bring himself to lie to the only teacher he'd ever respected. Slowly, he nodded his head.

Mr. Hodges raised his eyebrows, looked him up and down, reappraising him; then, with almost silent steps, he continued his way up the column of desks.

EIGHT O'CLOCK: **Blowback for Cynthia**

Cynthia gripped the knob of Paul's front door, but it didn't turn. She knocked, but nobody answered. There was a key hidden by the back door, so she walked down the porch steps and along the driveway. As soon as she opened the gate in the stockade fence, she saw a pile of junk on the deck. One of her photo albums lay beside her pet rabbit's cage, tipped sideways on a heap of clothes. High heels were strewn all over the deck like fallen leaves.

"What the fuck?"

Cynthia hurried onto the deck and noticed that the cage door was open. Her rabbit was gone.

"Mr. Peabody?" Her voice quivered. "Mr. Peabody?"

She tried the back door to the house, but it was locked, and the key was not in its hiding place. She banged on the door. "What's going on?" she screamed. Through the door's window, she could see the staircase leading up to Paul's room. She yanked on the knob, her breath rasping with sobs. She realized that Paul must have thrown all her stuff right down the stairs and out onto the deck while she was at work. No conversation. No fight. No warning.

Spotting a patch of white in the heap of clothes, she kneeled down to wrap Mr. Peabody in her arms. He nuzzled her hands then tucked his head inside her jacket. Cynthia sat down in the nest of clothes and cried. She called Paul's cell phone but only got his voice mail, so she called the store where he worked.

"Hello, Feed Barn."

"Can I talk to Paul, please?"

"Hang on." A brief pause. "Who is this?"

"Cynthia."

"He can't come to the phone right now. I'll tell him you called." *Click.*

Why won't you talk to me? She texted him.

Why did you throw me out? She was crying hysterically.

What did I do wrong? She sucked air like a drowning child.

Cynthia searched her mind for some clue to understanding. Paul was leaving for UConn at Storrs in a few days, but they hadn't talked about breaking up. She bought him skis and lift tickets as a going-away present, and he bought her a laptop for her classes at Naugatuck. They were going to see each other on weekends. Why did he do this?

Was it the drugs? Cynthia quit cold turkey after Six Flags, but Paul kept getting drunk, high, rolling, and tripping, and he wanted Cynthia to keep up with him. When she refused, he held it against her. Cynthia had been warned by her therapist that her attempts to help Paul only distracted her from helping herself while also denying Paul's power to help himself. The more he realized he needed her, the more he resented her. He called her a phony, a puppet. He said that her shrink was filling her head with bullshit.

Cynthia's therapist had given her a book called *Women Who Love Too Much* by Robin Norwood. The stories in the book mirrored her parents' marriage perfectly, and Cynthia came to understand how she was trapped in the same cycle. Her dad was an alcoholic, always putting her mom down, but she made excuses for him, tried to heal him. Just like Paul was addicted to substances and treated Cynthia terribly. But she kept believing he would change, couldn't imagine life without him. All her expectations were tied up with Paul, and she kept trying to fix their dysfunctional relationship instead of trying to fix herself.

She remembered the book and stopped crying. She looked at the screen of her phone. *Why won't you talk to me? Why did you throw me out? What did I do wrong?* She was doing it again, focusing on repairing the perpetually broken connection between them. She was "loving him too much," no matter how little he loved her. She was blaming herself, when he deserved the blame.

Cynthia sniffed hard and got up. She dropped Mr. Peabody into his cage, dragged it off the heap, and studied the pile. It contained all her worldly possessions. Dumped in a mess like that, it all looked so meaningless. Why did she have so many shoes? She thought of the street people in New York City, pushing around their shopping carts of worthless junk. For a moment she wanted to walk away and leave it all. The thought was thrilling, liberating. But she needed to work tomorrow, and she had a lot to do before then.

She opened her phone again but closed the text thread. She called home.

"Mom? Can you come pick me up?"

EIGHT O'CLOCK: **Result**

When the hero claims the Treasure, he or she triggers some Result before returning to the ordinary world. Theseus slays the Minotaur and saves the lives and dignity of future Athenians, but angers King Minos as a Result. He must flee home to Athens before he is arrested. King Minos's daughter, Ariadne, helps Theseus and his countrymen escape by ship, and she joins them. They stop en route at the island of Naxos to celebrate Theseus's successful quest, his love for Ariadne, and their escape from death in the Minotaur's labyrinth. Theseus has won the day, but the Olympian gods will balance the scales. In the confusion of the next day's launch, Ariadne is left on Naxos as the ships sail for Athens. Theseus returns home as Athens's greatest hero, but he pays a heavy price: his beloved.

In the Hunger Games' aftermath, Katniss Everdeen's bold refusal to bow to the gamemasters' fickle commands in the game's finale Results in civil unrest throughout the twelve subjugated districts of

Panem. As revolution brews, Caesar Flickerman interviews Katniss on television, President Snow interrogates her in private, and Peeta questions her in secret. All of them want to know her true feelings. She sticks to her story of desperate love, but not even Katniss knows for sure. With her heart and Panem in turmoil, she rides the train home to District 12.

After distributing Treasures to Dorothy and her friends, the Wizard of Oz departs in his hot air balloon along with Dorothy and Toto. At the last moment, Toto jumps out, and Dorothy chases after him. In the original book, the friends endure more hardships on their journey to Glinda the Good Witch, but the Result is the same as in the movie. Glinda reveals that Dorothy has possessed the power to return home all along. It is contained within the magic slippers.

Colin's and Cynthia's Results are similar to Dorothy's epiphany: "I can save myself." The callous rejection by Colin's biological father could have thrown his life into confusion, but it actually stabilized it by eliminating the major unknown variable that had caused his disequilibrium. In the wake of that clarification, Colin fortifies his social identity with renewed certainty—the prankster, the smart aleck who really is smarter than you. When his math teacher, Mr. Hodges, redirects that energy, Colin's productivity improves exponentially. By exorcising his spectral father, Colin surges ahead to the next phase of his Hero's Journey: college.

Cynthia survives a terrifying day trip that shreds her feet along with her fanatic devotion to Paul. As she watches him con himself and his father into believing he will change, she awakens from his spell. As a Result, her therapy sessions allow her to clearly see herself and the clockworks of her own heart. She realizes she and Paul are repeating her parents' dysfunctional relationship: the addict and his enabling, sympathetic lover. Yet before she builds up the courage to leave Paul, he exiles her.

Curiously, the hero is not the main actor during the eight o'clock hour. This stage of the Hero's Journey is dominated by the consequences of his or her deeds, the universe's backlash. In that way, it mirrors its opposite number on the clock face: four o'clock, when the hero overcame his or her initial Trials upon entering the special world. Now the hero must navigate back across that inhospitable terrain, passing through the aftermath of a successful quest.

Returning to your own life experience, what happened after you claimed that Treasure following your moment of truth? Were you swept smoothly back to your comfort zone? Or did you deal with some blowback? Before the smoke cleared and the dust settled, you probably had to iron out some wrinkles caused by the big event.

This is perhaps the hardest stage for teenagers to manage because they tend to fixate so purely on the Treasure at stake, whether academic, athletic, romantic, or some other prize. The following hour rolls out the ripple effects two, three, or more waves beyond the central cause. Failure might open the door to a missed opportunity, or success might yield unforeseen costs, as for Theseus. Most importantly, a young hero's own emotions might take her by surprise. Helping her untangle and validate those feelings is part of a mentor's important role.

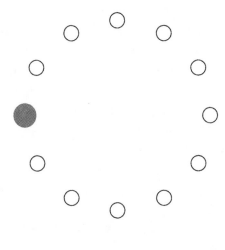

CHAPTER 9

Return

A t three o'clock in this cycle, the hero left the boundaries of his
or her ordinary world. At nine o'clock he or she returns home.
Peter, Susan, Edmund, and Lucy tumble out of the magical wardrobe.
Katniss Everdeen returns to District 12 after her victory in the Hunger
Games. Jack climbs down the beanstalk and then destroys it.

NINE O'CLOCK: **Colin 2.0**

Colin wedged his duffel bag full of clothes above his minifridge in the
back of a borrowed Chevy Blazer.

"I hope that's everything. There's no room for anything else," his
Aunt Lee said.

"You've got your toothbrush?" his mom asked.

Colin pulled it out of his pocket.

"Let's get you to college, big man," Kelly said and walked around
to the driver's door. Aunt Lee elbowed some bags aside in the backseat

and climbed in. Colin took one last look at the little blue bungalow, a last whiff of the fecund reservoir. He patted the roof of his mangled red Honda. It had gotten him back and forth to work all summer, even after he was rear-ended. The insurance company gave him almost four grand to fix the damage, but he spent the money on school supplies instead. That accident had basically paid for everything from a toaster oven to a fully loaded Dell PC.

Colin jumped into the passenger seat as his mom and aunt sang along to the classic rock station. He leaned toward the open window, letting the breeze ruffle his hair, and watched his neighborhood slide by. Past all the places where he'd played touch football, street hockey, and manhunt. Past all the houses on his school bus's route, one by one. Two songs later they were merging with the highway's northbound traffic. Colin could see his high school up on the hill, dominating the valley. His friends would all be getting their new class schedules and locker assignments next week—he would be at college.

They drove north up Interstate 87, past Albany and Lake George, then took the two-lane highway past Oscar's Adirondack Smoke House and Gore Mountain Ski Resort, threading through hours of towering pines that faded out along the Raquette River near Potsdam. Those city streets brought them to Clarkson University's main entrance. Kelly turned into the manicured campus and followed their handwritten directions to Farrisee dorm.

Colin led the way to his room on the second floor and walked in the open door. The young man inside was much shorter than Colin. A white T-shirt and pajama pants covered his bony frame.

"Hey. I'm Colin, your new roommate."

"Hello. I'm Chidozi Checklameka Ategwu."

"Hey, Chidozi."

"Please, call me Dodo."

Dodo came from Nigeria by way of New Jersey. Their two suitemates arrived while Colin was unloading the truck. Brian had brown hair and a cultivated soul patch on his chin. He wore corduroys and a Phish T-shirt. He'd seen plenty of jam band shows growing up near hippie New Paltz. Eddie arrived wearing a Hawaiian shirt, khaki shorts, and a broad smile. His light brown hair sat in tangles on his square head.

Colin's mom and aunt left for the parent reception when the dorm's resident assistant gathered all the students together in their floor's common room. There were twelve boys and four girls assigned to four suites on the floor, plus the RA in his single room. Each suite comprised two bedrooms sandwiching a private bathroom. Everyone sat on the chairs, couches, or floor and discreetly checked one another out while their thin, blond RA explained the rules.

"This dorm is just for schoolies. That's what you are: students in the Clarkson School program, finishing your high school credits while taking your freshman-level courses. I was a schoolie two years ago, so I know what it's like. Come to me if you have any questions. There are about a thousand regular freshmen this year, and they'll be moving into the dorms in the Reynolds quad next week. You'll be mixed in all the same classes with them, but they won't party with you, so don't even try. You guys aren't even eighteen yet, so if you get busted for alcohol, you're in big trouble, along with anyone who gives it to you. There's also a curfew for schoolies in the first semester. You need to be back on this floor by two o'clock in the morning."

"That seems like a stupid rule," Colin whispered to Dodo. "Why wouldn't you be back by two o'clock?"

Dodo shrugged his shoulders.

"What was that?"

"Nothing." Colin said.

"Why don't we introduce ourselves so we can call each other by name? Go ahead and start us off."

Colin stood up, realizing that he was a perfect stranger to these people, just as they were unknown to him. Apart from the three guys next to him, nobody even knew his name. He could tell them anything, and they'd believe it. This was a novel situation for Colin. He'd lived in the same town all his life and rarely met a kid he didn't already know through school, church, sports, or by reputation. That kid pooped his pants in fourth grade. That girl got drunk at her sister's graduation party. That guy deals pot. Colin McIntyre, the smart aleck with no dad.

But now he had a blank slate. He was starting from scratch.

"I'm Colin McIntyre and, yes, this is my natural hair color."

"Hi, Colin. What's your hometown?" The RA prompted.

"Monroe, New York, near the Jersey border."

"Welcome to Clarkson. Who's next?"

Nobody asked about his parents. Nobody even cared.

As Dodo introduced himself, Colin looked at the eyes of the other students. They were only half listening, accepting everything at face value while mentally scripting their own introductions. This was a new beginning for everyone, a chance to be who they always wanted to be.

• • •

Within a few weeks, the semester was fully under way. The schoolies really weren't welcome at parties, because the older students feared expulsion if they gave them alcohol. With that popular activity eliminated, these high school–age engineering students spent a lot of time on their computers, downloading music and movies, playing video games, and chatting online. Colin and his friends rearranged the furniture in their suite to match their mismatched sleep habits. One room became a dark sleeping cave filled with all their beds; the other double became an office with all four desks. The hallway door to that room was always open, and at least one suitemate was always working on schoolwork or surfing the web, so the space evolved into an informal computer lab and social magnet for the whole floor. People showed up with their laptops to collaborate on assignments or watch movies together.

The few girls in Colin's classes were smart and funny, and there was plenty of clever banter, but Colin was afraid to take the next step. By the time he worked up his nerve to ask about their plans for the weekend, they always had a date. The girls on his floor were busy most weekends because one of them had a brother in a fraternity. Clarkson's male-female ratio was three-to-one, so the girls had plenty of invitations. Colin's suitemate Eddie was lucky enough to start dating another schoolie within the first weeks of term, and soon spent every night in her room.

The first big change in Colin's social life came when he was recruited by the rugby team. At six feet, three inches tall, he fit right in. They didn't have a coach, so the team captains organized their matches against other colleges. Practices were grueling, and one afternoon the new players had to pass the initiation rite known as "beer laps."

Colin and the other rookies raced around the field as their teammates cheered from one goal or ran alongside them. When they completed the first lap, a mug of warm beer greeted each of them.

"Chug! Chug! Chug!"

They chugged.

"Run! Run!" The upperclassmen ran them hard for a second lap, and Colin felt the suds in his stomach churning into foam. He got to the goal and chugged the next beer. He was halfway around when the first mouthful of hot beer rose up out of his stomach. He leaned over the sideline and spit it into the grass. As he looked back, another rookie tossed up his own pint. Colin watched it spray over a third runner. "This is so stupid." Colin said. He laughed at the idiocy and kept running. Eight laps and eight beers later, he was exhausted and very drunk. He bent over and retched beside the other rookies while their new teammates cheered and showered them with even more beer.

The practices were more focused on the sport after that, and everyone usually went back to the rugby team's town house afterward. The veterans made the rookies drink beer out of an old rugby boot and some other stupid things like that, but they were always protective of Colin. Nobody wanted a call from the dean.

Their third game was at home, and they beat their crosstown rival, SUNY Potsdam. Colin was muddy and sore as he walked toward the parking lot.

"Hey, Colin. Good game today." The team captain popped him in the shoulder.

"Thanks. Have fun tonight." Colin knew there would be a party at the town house.

"Hit the showers and then come over."

"Seriously? I'm a schoolie, remember?"

"I don't give a shit what you are. We couldn't have won today without your tackle in the third. See you later." He winked and climbed into his car. Colin waved and hustled across the lot toward his dorm, feeling a little less sore.

That night, Colin got a taste of real college life. The basement of the town house was jammed with people holding plastic cups. Christmas lights and loud music electrified the room. Experts played beer pong and flip cup, but Colin didn't dare attempt those games. His teammates kept filling his cup, and pretty soon he lost track of how many he'd had. It felt great to be accepted, to be a member of this tribe. He felt so comfortable, so relaxed. The conversation flowed easily, even when he chatted with a few older girls. He felt every inch a champion as he walked home that night, dizzy with possibilities.

As he approached the door to Farrisee dorm, somebody stepped into his path.

"Hey, Colin. How are you doing?"

"Hey, what's up?" It was his RA, smoking a cigarette.

"It's kind of late. Where have you been?"

"Nowhere, just out, you know."

"Rugby house had a party tonight, didn't they?"

"I don't know."

"You're on the team, aren't you? You would know."

"Right, well, I'm going to bed."

"It's after two o'clock Colin."

Colin walked around him. "That's why I'm going to bed. See ya."

● ● ●

On Tuesday Colin found himself in the office of the director of the Clarkson School. He had short gray hair and seemed too small for his massive desk. Dark wood panels covered the walls, and heavy curtains framed the tall windows.

"Colin, why don't you tell me what happened on Saturday night?"

"I came back to the dorm after two o'clock."

"And you understood the two o'clock curfew during fall semester for schoolies?"

"Yeah, I just lost track of time. I'm sorry. It won't happen again."

"Where were you until so late at night? What were you doing?"

"I was just hanging out with friends."

"Were you at the party with the rugby team?"

"Not the whole time, but yeah, I was there."

"Some of those students are over twenty-one, and I'm sure there was alcohol at the party. Did any of them serve you alcohol?"

"No. They told me I was a schoolie, so I couldn't have any."

"So, you were the only person at that party not drinking alcohol? Until two-thirty in the morning?"

"I probably wasn't the only person."

"Colin, we take this elite program very seriously. You were among only seventy high school students worldwide to be elevated directly into college-level academics after eleventh grade, but not all of college life is available to you as a schoolie. You've made a poor decision in testing that boundary. I've informed the rugby team captain that you are off the team. Furthermore, your two o'clock curfew will be extended through the spring semester. If you want to remain at Clarkson, I suggest you focus on your studies and not on extracurricular activities. Are we clear?"

"Yes."

"Good. You have great potential, or you wouldn't be here. Let's put this incident behind us." He rose and extended his hand.

"Okay. Thank you." Colin shook his hand and walked out. On his way across the main lawn back toward Farrisee dorm, he cursed the stupid rules. He cursed his RA for ratting him out. He cursed his luck for walking home at just the right time to get caught. But before he even reached his dorm, he stopped cursing and realized that he'd almost blown it. He'd almost lost his golden ticket and been sent home in disgrace. If that happened, all those naysayers for all those years would shake their heads with that same sanctimonious explanation: "What do you expect? He's got no dad."

Colin couldn't stand the thought of that.

NINE O'CLOCK: **Cynthia Steps Back**

Cynthia stepped into the pharmacy's back office—a cramped, white-washed room with barely enough space for a desk and file cabinet, now crowded with three people. She shook hands with Diana, who had bought the pharmacy last month. Cynthia had seen Diana a few times, always dressed to the nines and usually with a phone in her hand, but she'd never really talked to her. She wore designer eyeglasses and fancy diamond earrings.

"Hello, Cynthia. Thanks for coming in today."

"How's it going, Cynthia?" Dave, the store manager, gave her a warm handshake and a big smile. He was never this friendly.

Diana sat down. "Before we start, I'd just like to ask if there's anything you'd like to tell us."

Cynthia felt a flash of panic but presented a confused expression. "About what?" she asked. Cynthia had stopped stealing after Six Flags, months before Diana bought the shop.

"Anything at all. We wanted to give you the chance to speak freely. Is there something on your mind? Something you'd like to get off your chest?"

She knows something. "I really like working here. Is that what you mean?" Cynthia had heard that whenever Diana bought a business, she laid people off then sold the place within a year.

"Cynthia, what do you know about the store's security system?" Dave asked.

Cynthia's legs tightened. Her uncertainty was genuine, but sharper than she tried to show. "Nothing, I guess. I don't even have keys."

Dave smiled and nodded, but Diana's eyes never left Cynthia's. "As part of the purchase process, we took inventory and audited the last twelve months of sales. We noticed some discrepancies. Would you care to comment on that?"

If she knows, why doesn't she just call the police? "I don't know what all that means." Cynthia said.

Diana leaned in. "Store property is missing. There's a clear pattern of shrink."

Cynthia knitted her brow. "You mean shoplifting? I didn't see any-thing." Cynthia kept thinking about the security system. *What security system? It must be a bluff. She's fishing for a confession.*

Silence.

Diana smiled. "Thank you for being so candid. We're still gather-ing information as we try to better understand this situation. In any case, we've made some decisions about staffing, and I'm sorry to tell you that your position has been eliminated. You're not being fired for cause, but we do have to let you go for budgetary reasons."

"Sorry, Cynthia. Let me know if you need a reference." Dave said.

"We'll pay you for the rest of the week, but you can take those days off. Good luck, Cynthia." Diana rose and extended her hand. Cynthia shook her hand and Dave's and then hurried out, avoid-ing eye contact with her coworker who was ringing up a customer. Cynthia stayed composed until she closed her car door, then cursed in a whispered mantra as the questions flooded through her mind. *Am I busted? Should I have acted more upset? Or less confused? Do they really have a security system?*

* * *

Cynthia poured coffee into a mug and added sugar. Her dad had already left for work, and her mom was watching TV in her bedroom. Leaning against the kitchen counter, she remembered high-school mornings, getting her things together and waiting for a ride from her brother. Things were so much simpler then.

She'd been living at home for a few weeks, and her mom was thrilled to have her back. Her dad avoided her. Cynthia kept up with her classes at Naugatuck and found a new job at the Ground Round. Other cashiers at the pharmacy had lost their jobs too, and Dave was practically running the store alone. Cynthia filled Mr. Peabody's water bottle and carried it upstairs with her coffee.

She'd just slipped the metal straw through the bars of her rab-bit's cage when the doorbell rang. Cynthia's friends always texted her before they dropped by, so she let her mom answer the door. Cynthia was shuffling through some of the clothes in her closet when her mom called her name. She started down the stairs in her pajamas and peeked around the corner at the landing. Two women in pantsuits stood beside her mom in the front hall.

"Hi." Cynthia said. Her mom didn't say anything, but Cynthia read danger in her expression.

"Hi, Cynthia. I'm Special Agent Clark and this is Agent Wyant. We're from the Drug Enforcement Administration. We'd like to ask you a few questions."

Cynthia felt her skin shrink. She started to say "I need to get dressed" so that she could flush her stash, but then she remembered that she didn't have any drugs in her room. Even the lipstick-size Tylenol tube in her purse held no Ecstasy. She stuttered for a second and then descended the stairs, trying to look bewildered and blameless.

"We're investigating the handling of controlled substances at the Village Pharmacy. You worked there until recently, correct?" Agent Clark asked.

"Yes."

"Were you working there last summer during the month of June?"

"Yeah."

Agent Wyant held a manila folder as though she were reading a magazine folded back, then she flipped the cover to display a large black-and-white photograph attached to the inside. Cynthia felt the heat drain from her face. The photo showed Cynthia at the pharmacy's lab counter with her hand in a white paper bag.

"Is that you in the picture?" asked Agent Clark.

"I guess so." Cynthia's bladder threatened to spill.

"What are you doing in the picture?"

"It's a little fuzzy. Putting something in a bag, it looks like."

"Putting something in? Or taking something out?"

Cynthia felt goose bumps rise on her neck. Agent Wyant pushed the photo closer to Cynthia while studying her reaction.

"I can't tell."

"You must tell me, Cynthia. This is a federal investigation and—"

"No, I mean it's not clear from the picture if I'm putting stuff in or taking stuff out."

"Did you ever remove anything from a customer's bag?"

"Yeah, sure, to check the label or something."

"Why would you do that, check the label?"

"If the pharmacist told me to, I guess."

"How often did you remove medication from a bag for those reasons?"

"I don't know. That was back in June."

"How often did you find yourself handling controlled substances while unsupervised?"

"There was always a pharmacist there."

"I don't see one in that photo." Agent Wyant moved it even closer.

"Well, he could be over here." Cynthia pointed outside the frame.

"Could be?"

"Yeah, or he could be in the office."

"So, there were times that you were in that area alone, times when you removed items from customers' bags without supervision?"

"I don't know. Maybe."

"How often were you in that area alone?"

"A few times a week, I guess."

"You're currently taking Klonopin, correct?"

Cynthia was startled. "Yeah. To help me sleep."

"Did you ever handle your own medication without direct supervision?"

"No. I get it filled at another pharmacy."

Agent Clark looked at Cynthia for a moment, then at the picture, then at Agent Wyant, who slipped it into her folder and held Cynthia's eyes.

"Cynthia, as part of this investigation, I need to ask you a direct question." Her voice was husky and forceful. "If you give a false or misleading statement, you could face charges, so answer truthfully. Do you understand?"

"Yes."

"Did you ever illegally remove a controlled substance from the pharmacy?"

Cynthia shook her head, appearing scandalized. "No."

"You never skimmed any pills?"

"No." Cynthia looked at each agent, then at her mother, trying to weigh their doubt. The silence stretched, and Cynthia resisted the urge to fill it.

"Thank you both for your cooperation with this ongoing investigation. If there's anything either of you want to tell us—anything you forgot to mention—please get in touch." Agent Clark handed her business card to Cynthia and her mom, then everyone shook hands and said good-bye.

After the door closed, Cynthia's mom locked eyes with her.

"What?" Cynthia asked.

"Is this why you lost your job at the pharmacy?"

"Mom, they laid off a bunch of people, not just me." Her mom held her gaze. "Mom . . ." They both noticed the dark DEA sedan leave the driveway and cruise down the hill. When Cynthia turned back to face her mom, she found herself unable to finish her sentence. While she was living with Paul, she had talked to her mom several times a week. They both complained about the men in their lives, and Cynthia tried to pass along what she was learning from *Women Who Love Too Much*. She told her mom about everything Paul did wrong, but left out her own misdeeds. It was easy to do on the phone, but looking her mom in the eye, Cynthia couldn't bring herself to lie.

"Mom, do you remember when I went to the Dominican Republic?"

"Yeah."

"I paid for that with . . ." Cynthia looked at the floor, unable to watch comprehension dawn across her mother's face.

"You were stealing drugs from the pharmacy."

Cynthia nodded, watching her tears hit the wood floor between her feet.

"Cynthia, that picture—"

"No!" Cynthia interrupted, meeting her mom's eyes. "I stopped after Six Flags. I swear! They must have put that camera in after Diana bought the pharmacy."

Her mom looked through her. "Are you using drugs?"

Cynthia straightened. "No, Mom. I haven't since Six Flags. I'm done with all that." Saying the words out loud, Cynthia heard the weight behind them. Her mom heard it too.

NINE O'CLOCK: **Return**

The hero's Return is easy to spot in the typical monomyth. Where did the story begin? In the hero's hometown. When does the hero return to that location? At nine o'clock in the cycle. Of course that physical Return metaphorically represents an emotional return to a feeling of security. Theseus beaches his ship in Athens, Dorothy awakens in Kansas, and Bilbo Baggins returns to the Shire.

Cynthia's journey also comes full circle. She was finishing high school when she began her long, slow trajectory away from her parents' care, like the shining metal marble in a pinball machine, drifting slowly into contact with several shocking events that tossed her in unpredictable directions. Finally, after all the bells and flashing lights along her dizzying, whiplash path, she drifted slowly back home, much the worse for wear.

Some stories don't offer such an obvious physical parallel to the hero's interior journey. But even when the hero doesn't return to his geographic starting point, his quest has clearly run its course. *The Odyssey* begins with Odysseus in a static situation on Calypso's island, and he returns to a similarly stable position in the final pages. Luke Skywalker doesn't go back to his aunt and uncle's ruined farm on Tatooine, but he finds an emotional home among his new comrades.

Colin follows a pattern similar to Luke's. Instead of a literal homecoming, Colin crosses a figurative threshold back into the ordinary world of self-assurance, leaving the territory of social stigma. His quest for wholeness began when his kindergarten classmates made Father's Day cards all around him and he deduced that his family was missing an essential piece. But in college, nobody even asked if your parents were still together. That piece ceased to be essential, so Colin could leave his anxiety in the past and accept a new worldview.

What about you? When did you last return from a trip outside your comfort zone? What about your teens? When did they last set foot on firm ground after a period of time on choppy seas?

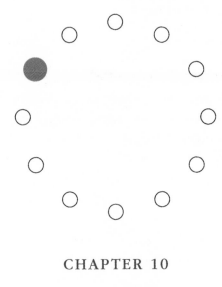

CHAPTER 10

New Life

The recent journey has transformed the hero into a new person. Theseus returns to Athens with good news for his father, but King Aegeus is dead. Marty McFly marvels at his family's prosperity when he returns to his home and time in *Back to the Future*.

TEN O'CLOCK: **Colin Meets Ashley**

On New Year's Eve, Colin left the bungalow wearing a plaid flannel shirt and a down jacket, both Christmas gifts from his mom. She was working as a teacher in the Chester public schools now. She had her own sixth-grade classroom in the same town where she used to pack circuit breakers for the phone company. Colin drove her old Honda down the familiar stretch of road. How many times had he passed this way on his bike or on the bus back and forth to school?

He turned onto Laroe Road and pulled off at Lisa Katmarski's house. Amet and Sanjay were already there, along with a bunch of girls. Last year their clique had been a bunch of guys hanging out playing video games and backyard sports. This year, as high school seniors, Sanjay and Amet were hanging out with girls. Over the last few days, Colin had adjusted to their new social reality. This was a small gathering, only about eight people. Clair, Ashley, Lisa, and Laura were there—girls they'd known for years from the school bus and their classes. Everyone was relaxing, sitting around the TV and talking. Colin sat next to Ashley. He'd always considered her completely out of his league.

"I like her shoes." Ashley said. Alicia Keys was on the screen, singing in front of her piano for a huge outdoor crowd in New York City.

"Oh, man, I love those shoes." Colin said. "That's so great. I can't believe we both have such great taste in shoes. We have so much in common."

Ashley chuckled.

They continued to banter about the stage sets and costumes, and as the earth gently swung into a fresh circuit around the sun, gravity pulled them closer together on the couch. Before Colin went home, he had Ashley's number.

He texted her the next day. "I had a lot of fun at the party last night. We should hang out sometime before I go back to school."

"Or like a million times," she replied.

Ashley had classes that week, but Colin visited her house on Friday night. He'd seen her family's fancy colonial home before, but never imagined that he'd go inside. He parked in front of their three-car garage and followed Ashley to the home theater in their basement. They watched *Titanic* with the lights out and a bowl of popcorn on her lap. The sofa seemed to sink toward the middle. Apart from that interrupted moment with Danielle during the eighth-grade dance, Colin had never kissed a girl before. What if she didn't want him to? What if she did want him to, but he did it wrong? If he turned his head toward her, it would be too obvious. Moving only his eyes, Colin risked a glance.

The scattered blue light from the television flickered on her face, accenting the silhouette of her long eyelashes blooming from the shadow of her eye. A fragment of light glimmered in that darkness, drawing Colin toward it. The television's frantic fiddles kept pace with his pulse. Ashley looked away from the TV into his eyes. Their faces hung there a moment, pale in the electric glow. Then Ashley's eyelashes folded together. Their lips touched as Jack and Rose danced on tables in the *Titanic*'s belly. Nothing had ever felt so right.

• • •

During the spring term, they talked every day. They chatted online, texted, and called each other. Colin had bought a used car so that he could visit her on weekends until Clarkson finished in May. Ashley walked to her car one afternoon in the high school parking lot, and there were flowers under the windshield wipers of her green Jetta.

When Colin returned home in May, Ashley still had a month left of her junior year. He worked at the Tuxedo Club, but they spent every other minute together. Afternoon drives up to Bear Mountain State Park, weekend parties at a friend's house, and then Colin's senior prom in June. Technically, his freshman year at Clarkson also counted toward his high school diploma, so he graduated with his old classmates.

Colin wore a black tux, black shirt, and white silk bow tie to the prom. His red hair was shaved to stubble at the neck, fading up to a three-quarter-inch buzz on top. On his feet he wore a brand-new pair of black Nikes with a white swoosh. He parked on the street in front of a friend's house where everyone was gathering for pictures. Amet was already there, tossing his overnight bag into the twenty-passenger limousine they'd hired.

"Did you bring it?" Amet asked.

Colin unzipped his backpack to show Amet the vodka and whiskey inside. The bartender at the Tuxedo Club had hooked him up.

Another friend leaned in. "That's what I'm talking about!" He high-fived Colin. They left their bags in the limo and lined up for photos. Ashley was wearing a black-and-white Kate Spade cocktail dress and holding a clutch purse. She blushed a little when she saw him. Tonight was the night.

"Hey, what's this?" The limo driver called out to Colin, holding up his backpack. All the parents stopped taking photos and looked. The limo driver pulled a vodka bottle out of the bag. "Hey, carrot-top. Are you twenty-one?"

Colin looked at the driver, then at his friends. Their parents were all glaring at him. The outlaw. The boy with no dad.

"That's a lot of booze." The driver pawed inside Colin's bag, the bottles clinking. "Smells like trouble."

Colin stepped over to him. "Come on, man. What are you doing? You can't go in my bag."

The driver kept his voice low. "You gonna get these girls drunk? Is that your plan?" And then louder, for the parents to hear, "I'll just keep this with me until I drop you off." He smirked at Colin and put the bag on the front seat of the limousine.

The photo session was tense after that. Couples posed while their parents took snapshots, and Colin heard them whispering about him, as they had all his life. It didn't touch him anymore. He was somebody else. They were living in his past, and he had already left it behind.

Everyone piled into the limo, and it rolled to the Ramada in Mahwah. By the time they arrived, the ballroom was flooded with glamour and hormones. All four hundred of Colin's classmates sported rented tuxedos and sumptuous gowns. They sang and danced to the recent top-forty hits, the soundtrack of their four-year high school prison term. The unrest between rival cliques dissolved into camaraderie as they shared a communal victory over the adults who had tried to tame them but failed.

By the time the DJ played the official prom song at the end of the night, Colin's shirt was soaked with sweat. Ashley's hair was flat, and her corsage was wilted. They pressed against each other in the warm crush of bodies, swaying in time. Colin rested his cheek against her forehead and his hands at the small of her back. Her fingers brushed the fuzz behind his ears, and she tipped her head back to look at him. Wordless anticipation passed between them. Music filled the humid ballroom, but they were oblivious to the crowd of silhouettes. They pressed together unashamed and kissed until the lights went up.

The driver held the limo door open, looking them over as they climbed inside. Before closing the door, he handed Colin his bag with a warning: "If anybody pukes, you're cleaning it up." On the way into Manhattan, they passed the bottles and retold their favorite stories bathed in the limo's multicolored light.

"Remember the fistfight in the lower parking lot?"

"Remember when Colin taught that math class?"

The radio station picked up Hot 97 FM as they got closer to New York and wove their way to Caroline's Comedy Club. They walked in wearing prom dresses and tuxedos, now riding a gentle buzz. They clustered around tables near the stage and tried to order more drinks. No dice. After watching stand-up routines for a couple hours, they rode back up along the Hudson River. The limo dropped them off at the same house well after midnight, and everyone parted ways. Colin drove away with Ashley in his red Honda Civic. Her parents knew she would be spending the weekend at the Jersey Shore with her girl-friends, but there were still a few hours before dawn.

Colin pulled up in front of his Aunt Lee's house. She had given him the keys so he could water the plants while she was out of town. He led Ashley around the house to the back deck. He dropped their bags and kissed her in the starlight and the humidity and the musk of azalea blooms. Then Colin stepped back and flipped off the hot tub lid with a magician's flourish, revealing a well of liquid light. Ashley giggled, and Colin spun her around to unzip her dress. She crossed her arms and searched the darkness for witnesses. As only the stars watched, she slipped from her cocktail dress and into the steaming water.

Colin watched her slide through the rippling glow, a dream made real. She resurfaced like a mermaid, slick and shimmering, her glis-tening face above the water's roiling surface. Colin unraveled his bow tie like a mystery, and his black clothes fell like shadows. Pale and completely exposed, he climbed into the bubbling water beside her, their faces uplit with turbulent swirls. They embraced as fireflies pulsed in the darkness. The crickets' chirping seemed to grow louder until Ashley's lips crept to Colin's ear. "Take me inside."

TEN O'CLOCK: **Cynthia's Future**

Cynthia lifted the stack of papers from her car and carried them against her chest like a pile of firewood. She pushed open the back door with her foot and rested her forearms on the kitchen counter before sliding them out from under her bulky criminology homework. The entire courtroom transcript from a murder trial rested on the counter. Her job was to read it and then write a persuasive essay in support of one side or the other, prosecution or defense.

Cynthia flipped through the first pages, the opening statements of both lawyers. The prosecution lawyer promised to prove means, motive, and opportunity. The defense attorney allowed that his client did kill the victim, but in an act of self-defense, not murder. Cynthia dug deeper into the transcript, bent over the counter and still wearing her coat. She pulled out a pen and circled the names of each witness the district attorney called, underlined parts of their testimonies, and made notes in the margins. She thought she could do a better job than that lawyer.

When she and Paul were dealing, they had a few friends who got caught. The legal system chewed them up and swallowed them, excreting them years later, hardened and broken. Cynthia feared that mysterious juggernaut, knowing that it might come for her any day, and she also resented it for being unjust, unnecessarily harsh. Her friends lost the best years of their lives as punishment for simply getting high. They hadn't hurt anyone. That's why she had decided to enroll in the Criminal Justice program at Naugatuck Valley Community College. Maybe she could help kids in a juvenile rehabilitation center or as a parole officer.

On top of that career plan, Cynthia worried about her own legal fate. She hadn't seen the DEA agents since their original visit, but she expected them to return any day. She deleted all her text and call history, purged her e-mail messages, and looked for other ways to cover her tracks. Every so often, an old buyer would ping her cell phone looking to score. When she mentioned that her phone might be tapped by the DEA, those conversations ended quickly.

Cynthia was already doing well at Naugatuck, better than she'd ever done in high school or in her interrupted semesters at Pace. She had pulled more than her own weight in the last group project, and her teacher had discreetly praised her for that. Ms. Bagnoli kept her dark, curly hair cut short. She always wore dressy pants with a button-down shirt and round glasses, wire-rimmed.

Their new project began with an identical stack of papers on each desk. At first Cynthia thought they were cinder blocks. All twenty-five students listened as Mrs. B explained the assignment. She told the class that reading the words of the transcript was the easy part. The hard part was getting into the mind of the accused. She wanted them all to be able to think like a criminal. Cynthia glanced around the room full of aspiring cops and prison guards. She felt like she had an unfair advantage.

As she read the defendant's personal testimony, she had no trouble getting inside his head. What the district attorney had described as a sudden, aggressive attack sounded more like a fight for his life when the defendant described it. They were both drunk and started quarreling. The victim pulled a knife and the defendant grabbed a shovel. Who drew first? They both ended up in the hospital, but only one walked out. Cynthia's heart broke when she read that they had been lifelong friends, had even been arrested together in high school.

Cynthia wrote her persuasive essay as the defense attorney, focusing on the relationship between the defendant and the deceased. She also cited the hospital and coroner reports, highlighting the multiple injuries the defendant suffered versus the few he caused. Simple arithmetic indicted the dead man as the attacker. Finally she drew attention to the deceased's record of violent behavior, contrasting it with the defendant's history of opportunistic but nonviolent crimes. She imagined herself standing before the jury, convincing them that a drunken argument between friends had blown up when the chronic brawler had pulled a knife, and that the pacifist had protected himself with tragic results. Live by the sword, die by the sword.

Ms. Bagnoli loved it and suggested that Cynthia transfer to Western Connecticut State University and then apply to law school. Cynthia laughed, but her old dream of studying at New York University came back to her. They had a strong program and a great alumni network. Five years from now, she could be a public defender for the City of New York. Cynthia could already see herself in an NYU sweatshirt.

TEN O'CLOCK: **New Life**

After returning to his ordinary world, the hero needs to reintegrate. Joseph Campbell used the phrase "master of the two worlds" to describe the hero's New Life. He has proved his mastery of the fearsome territory where he accomplished his quest, and that achievement has transfigured his position in society.

After twenty years abroad, Odysseus reclaims control of Ithaca. His cunning ideas during the siege of Troy are well known, including his Trojan Horse gambit. He returns to his throne with two decades of hard-won wisdom and glory, the model of ancient Greek ingenuity and resilience. Theseus is not so fortunate. He approaches Athens, still grieving the loss of Ariadne. In his grief he forgets to change the dark sail, indicating failure. King Aegeus, believing that Theseus has died with the tributes, commits suicide before the boat touches shore.

Katniss Everdeen made a living by hunting, gathering, and bartering before the Hunger Games. After surviving that ordeal, her New Life involves a luxurious home, plenty of food, and nationwide fame. When his quest is complete, Frodo Baggins awakens in Gondor and proceeds to a ceremony where he and Sam are glorified in song: "Praise them! The Ring-bearers, praise them with great praise!" Aragorn, in his own New Life as the King of Gondor, bows before them and places them on his throne to hear a minstrel recite the tale of "Frodo of the Nine Fingers and the Ring of Doom." Frodo has gained prestige, but it has cost him his innocence, the bloom of his youth, and the ring finger of his left hand. A big change from his old life as an ordinary hobbit in the Shire.

Cynthia lives her New Life in the same house where she started, but, like Frodo, much has changed inside her. She went to college but dropped out. She lived with Paul and got tossed out. She stole pills, dealt drugs, and was almost found out. Now on the other side of these experiences, she sees Paul more objectively, which helps her realize the same failings in herself. That awareness helps her break bad habits. Cynthia also grows through the sessions with her therapist. The patterns in her parents' marriage and her relationship with Paul seem so obvious and formulaic in hindsight. Cynthia's life experience injured her but advanced her maturity, something like the Norse god Odin's sacrificing of one of his eyes in exchange for a drink from the wisdom-granting waters in Mimir's Well.

Colin truly comes into himself at college. His personality had always been larger than life, and that bravado was originally a mask. Nevertheless, Colin eventually grows to fit it, gaining more and more confidence until he removes that veil at college, only to find that he is in fact the person he always pretended to be. When he sees his hometown friends over winter break, he really has outgrown his old life. Colin has become the master of two social worlds: college and his hometown. More importantly, he is now master of himself.

Colin is one of those heroes who can't fall in love until he resolves his internal issues. When he finally relaxes his guard, Colin realizes that his defensive posture is unnecessary. The world is ready to embrace him. In Malory's *Morte d'Arthur*, the Knights of the Round Table seek the Holy Grail, but they never encounter its grace through aggressive victory in arms. Quite the reverse. The Grail comes to them when they are wounded or supplicant. Only in a state of humility can they accept the mercy that will heal them. When Colin meets Ashley, he lets his armor fall away, and he is saved.

What about you? When did you return to a starting point and find that you had mastered a new level of your profession or a heretofore untamed aspect of yourself? What about your teens? What episodes have they experienced and grown from?

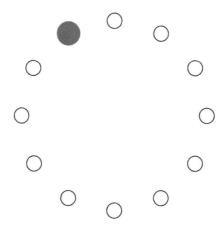

CHAPTER 11

Resolution

The hero's adventure has altered the course of events, which are resolved in this final hour of the cycle. Cinderella marries the prince. King Arthur dies after restoring peace to Britain. Simba and Nala baptize the next Lion King.

ELEVEN O'CLOCK: **Colin Understands**

Colin drove to Ashley's house straight from his job at the Tuxedo Club. Since prom, they'd spent every day together, almost like Colin was making up for all those years of being afraid to even talk to girls. All he wanted to do was be around her. And like children after a first taste of chocolate, they couldn't stop raiding the candy jar. Every time they got together—at his house, at her house, in his car—they shared that intimate ecstasy, that jarring consecration of young love.

Colin parked his beat-up Ford beside Ashley's shiny Jetta in her floodlit driveway. Her elegant home still seemed unattainable, like a castle at the top of a beanstalk. Ashley's mom opened the door as he approached. "Hi! Come on in, Colin."

"Thanks, Mrs. Godden. How are you today?"

"I'm fine. How was work?"

"It's a living." Colin knew he smelled like the smoky Golf House kitchen.

"Ashley's in her room. Go on upstairs."

"Thanks."

Colin ascended the staircase, planning to take Ashley out for ice cream at Mr. Cone. Then where could they go? His mom was home too. Maybe park by the lake.

"Hey, beautiful." Colin said, stepping through the doorway into Ashley's bedroom.

"Hi." She continued folding a pile of clothes on her floral bedspread.

Colin gave her a kiss on the cheek and sat on her bed. "What's wrong?"

"I'm fine," she said without meeting his eyes. Ashley's room had nine-foot ceilings and tall windows, framed by curtains and window scarves. The floors were polished wood, but the walls and furniture were white. Framed Renaissance prints hung on the walls instead of boy-band posters. She walked over to her bureau and slipped some folded clothes inside. The perfume bottles on the surface rattled when she closed the drawer.

"Are you sure? You seem kind of . . ." Colin said.

There was a huge closet with hanging bars on both sides and a rolling rack parked in between. She rolled the rack of clothes out into the room and disappeared into her closet. She came out with a few dresses on hangers and hung each one in a specific spot on the bar. Colin waited, wondering what could be bothering her. She would be leaving next week with her family to spend a month in Delaware. Maybe she was getting anxious about spending four weeks apart.

"Ashley, come on. You can tell me."

She crossed the room and pushed the bedroom door closed, silently turning the handle before releasing it, just as she had last week when her parents weren't home. Colin felt his body respond to that flash of memory—here in this room, on this bed. She didn't sit next to him now but stood in front of him with her arms crossed and said quietly, "I'm late."

It took Colin a moment to understand, then he stood and hugged her. Ashley was trembling. "It's okay. Don't worry about it. It doesn't mean anything. You'll get it any day," he said.

She pushed away from him. "You don't know that." She wiped her eyes.

"Well, you don't know either." He looked at the door and lowered his voice. "You're assuming that . . . it could be nothing. Just late, that's all."

Ashley picked up a blouse from the bed and snatched a bare hanger from the rack, "Or not." She wrestled the hanger into the blouse. "My parents could never know. If they ever found out . . ." She froze, her hands on the crossbar.

"Hold on. Slow down," Colin said. "How late are you?"

"Late enough."

"We could do a test."

"No." Ashley disappeared into the closet again.

Colin followed her, carefully touching her back as she hung up the blouse. "Ashley, we've been careful. I'm sure it's fine."

"How can you say it's fine? You're not taking this seriously!"

"I am. I just seriously think it's going to be fine."

She faced him, meeting his eyes for the first time that afternoon. "All I know is, I'm late. And there's only one reason why people are late."

Colin wrapped her in his arms, but her embrace was restrained. He had seen the blame in her eyes.

● ● ●

Colin drove home later that night, and his absolute optimism cracked when he considered the "what if" scenario. A cascade of realizations spilled through his mind. *This is exactly what my mom went through. This fear, this desperation. But she had no one to share it with. Ashley has her whole life ahead of her, all planned out. If she really is pregnant, is she going to have a baby in her senior year of high school? That's not happening. She won't make the same choice that my mom made. She's got AP classes next year and college plans. So she'll have the abortion, and that means some kid—some little clone of me—will never exist, never have me as a dad, never repeat this cycle, never accidentally get a girl pregnant and have these exact thoughts when he's my age. And if my mom had decided not to keep me, I wouldn't even be having these thoughts right now. I wouldn't be here at all. But my dad might have wanted my mom not to keep me, if he'd known. But I do know. But Ashley won't want a baby. That kid—my son or daughter—will never exist, and there's nothing I can do.*

The thoughts ricocheted around his skull, vibrating his bones. He stopped in front of his house and opened the driver's door in a daze. As he rose from the car, his legs gave out and he tumbled to his knees. Tears fell into the dust, and Colin realized he was crying, shaking. He leaned against the Ford's front tire and wrapped his arms around his shins. Sitting that midnight vigil, judged by the mocking frogs and impassive stars, Colin felt lost in the flood of consequences sweeping him into his future.

• • •

The next morning, Colin sat on a stool in Ashley's empty kitchen. On the way over, he'd stopped at Rite Aid. His heart raced as the old guy at the register rang up his bottle of Gatorade, bag of Doritos, and a home pregnancy test. Ashley was in the bathroom right now, learning their fate. Colin stared at the pile of junk mail on the granite countertop without seeing it. The trees outside the window stood perfectly still.

Ashley's dog drank from her dish beside the brushed-steel dishwasher, then sat down on Colin's foot and whined. Colin rubbed her ears. He dammed up his thoughts, waiting for Ashley to open the bathroom door.

He heard the click of the latch and Ashley's approaching footsteps. He stood up before Ashley rounded the corner into the kitchen.

"What does it say?"

She didn't look happy. Ashley held out the plastic stick, and Colin saw the result. One line. Negative. He let go of his grip on the stone counter and pulled her close.

"I still don't have my period. This could be wrong."

Colin gripped her shoulders and held her eyes with his. "Listen. This was a test, and we passed. If you stress out, that can make your period late, right? Stop worrying. These things are super accurate. It's science. You're not pregnant. You're fine." Colin trusted the chemistry, but Ashley's shoulders did not relax. He held her in the kitchen, hoping his confidence would infect her.

ELEVEN O'CLOCK: Cynthia Says Good-Bye

Cynthia pulled into the parking lot of the Feed Barn and switched off the engine. Her gut told her this was a mistake. Paul had been texting her for weeks, but Cynthia kept brushing him off. At first she didn't respond at all. After how he treated her, the way he ended things, he didn't deserve a reply. He apologized all over himself, day after day, and eventually she texted back. He wanted to see her again. Cynthia knew that was a bad idea, so she made excuses and kept her distance. Until yesterday. In a moment of weakness, she agreed to visit him at work during his lunch break. That seemed safe.

But now she was here, and the deepest part of her wanted to flee. That instinct tugged in her belly, and she felt the old thrill of doing something wrong, of going against all good sense. The same addiction to risk that had gotten her into so much trouble to begin with. She knew she should twist the ignition, start her car, and drive away. Instead she dropped the keys in her purse and opened the door.

Paul approached her as she crossed the parking lot, her heeled boots splashing the cold puddles. He carried his insulated lunch cooler in one hand.

"Hey." Paul hugged her, with his free arm.

"Hi." Cynthia leaned into him, then stepped back.

"Are you cold? Let's sit over here," Paul said.

They walked to a weathered wood picnic table, and Paul opened his cooler. "Want a beer?"

Cynthia's thrill evaporated. This meeting wasn't daring anymore, just pathetic. Last night Cynthia had wondered whether some vestigial undertow of her love for Paul might return and drag her back out to sea. It was easy to talk about their dysfunctional relationship in the safety of her therapist's office, but she feared love might blind her when she saw Paul in person. But she was seeing him clearly now. "No thanks," she said. "I can't stay long."

Paul popped the top of the can and took a long swig before meeting her eyes. He held her gaze and searched for something, but he didn't find it. "You're different," he said.

You're not, Cynthia thought, but she said, "So, how was Storrs?" Paul had left after a month, but he hadn't resumed classes at WestConn.

"Didn't work out." Paul swallowed the rest of the beer and traded it for a full can. He held another out to Cynthia. "You're sure?"

Cynthia shook her head. She felt sad for Paul's parents, who had believed in him, supported his plan for a fresh start. The memory of that night in the living room replayed in her mind, the desperation in Paul's voice, the tenderness in his dad's. Yet, here was the result. She stood up. "I have to go."

Paul's face softened, momentarily exposed. "Just like that? Just let it all go? How can you do that?"

"I'll never let go," Cynthia blurted, surprising herself. "But I have to move on, Paul. And you . . ." She caught herself, but finished the thought silently. *You're stuck.*

"What?"

"Good luck, Paul. I've got to go." Cynthia walked away and didn't look back.

• • •

A few days later, during Criminology class, Cynthia got another text from Paul.

Paul: "I know the other day you said you'd never let go and all, but being honest you have to. You're a very nice girl, but it's over for good. I'd actually rather not talk at this point. I never really wanted to try to get you back. I was trying to have lunch so we could establish a good long-lasting friendship, but you were always too busy, and it sucked that you would just lie about being too busy, but my intentions were never to try and get back with you. I was really hoping we could have a long and prosperous friendship, but you're not my good friend anymore. As a matter of fact, it was disappointing that you avoided me when we were supposed to be "best" friends, so this is my good-bye. I think it'd be straight if we didn't even converse."

Cynthia read it, thinking it seemed like a stretch, a petty attempt to have the last word and make himself out as the good guy. She wasn't going to be drawn into a quarrel. She wrote back: "Alright, bye."

"No hard feelings, Cynthia. I love you," Paul replied.

What bullshit, Cynthia thought. *Trying to take the high road after throwing my stuff on the porch when I wasn't even home, then leaving town for Storrs without a word. Didn't even have the balls to break up with me face to face.* "Yeah, right," she texted back.

"Doesn't mean I won't say 'hi' if I pass you."

What is he after? Some kind of Disney ending? She wrote back, "Fuck you. Don't say I love you."

"Had to fit in one last lie," Paul replied.

Exactly. Pure bullshit. "Yeah. I never lied and said I was too busy. I didn't want to talk to you and I should never have. Bye, Paul."

"Okay, it's like you said. It's better."

Why is he stringing this out? Why am I writing back? "I know," Cynthia responded, hoping that would be the end.

"I know you'll agree. I'm finally realizing it," Paul admitted.

"Thank God." Cynthia couldn't help herself.

"LOL. Cynthia it wasn't a lie that I love you. It's just not that love anymore. I don't take back anything of that relationship, and I'll hold it in my heart forever."

It's bullshit. It's bullshit. But what if it isn't? What if he really cares? Cynthia typed an ambiguous reply: "same."

"I love you, just not how I used to," Paul continued.

She wanted to stop herself. He'd been so bad to her, but the old feelings came back as tears. She broke her composure enough to put the truth into words. "But I know you'll never change into who I need you to be."

"I know."

"And we're in two separate places in life," she added.

"One thing I can admit for you: I've always had too much to work on and never was willing to take any steps, even after you put so much into changing. I apologize. I slowly ruined it all. I have to admit, I slowly ruined it all."

Cynthia looked at the words on her phone, perhaps the truest thoughts Paul had ever confessed. She couldn't think of anything more to say, and as she reread the screen with a mixture of nostalgia and vindication, she felt the moorings in her heart release. The screen blinked dark after a minute. It was the last time Cynthia ever heard from Paul.

ELEVEN O'CLOCK: **Resolution**

During this hour, a story's various plotlines resolve into conclusion. Cinderella's success in the special world of the royal ball leads to a wedding at eleven o'clock in the cycle. Luke Skywalker's struggles to save the galaxy and his father's soul both conclude with Darth Vader choosing good over evil, betraying the Emperor and sacrificing himself to save his son. During the Ewok victory party, the redeemed spirit of Luke's dad joins the ghostly forms of Yoda and Obi-Wan, smiling from the edge of the forest. The legend of King Arthur also culminates in a father-son battle, in which Arthur saves Britain by slaying his own misbegotten son. After Excalibur is returned to the magical waters of its origin and a dying Arthur sails away on a mystical barge, Malory's tale goes on to describe the fates of Guinevere, Lancelot, and the other knights. All the outstanding questions are settled in this last hour of the cycle.

Colin is finally secure enough in himself to be intimate with Ashley, but their brush with potential parenthood snaps a trip wire inside him. His newfound confidence crumbles under a complex avalanche of adult understanding. Their simple, tender acts of passion spin out in his mind, cycling through the endless consequences of generations of potential children. Ultimately Colin absorbs a richer comprehension of his mother's sacrifice and his own responsibilities as a sexually active young man.

Cynthia's problems with Paul, drugs, and crime were always symptoms of a deeper struggle against herself. Some insatiable part of her always yearned for bigger risks, sharper thrills. That impulsive bit of her personality led to her first rave and to everything that followed. The wiser side of Cynthia resisted the many reckless twists and turns along her journey but never won control. Finally the tables have turned. Cynthia is making good choices and mopping up the mess of her past. Her text message exchange with Paul illustrates her newfound clarity while revealing the endearing clumsiness of two young people trying to make sense of their muddled past.

This point of denouement represents an opportunity for reflection and interpretation. As mentors of adolescents, this is a time when we can inflect their comprehension of their recent adventure. We can ask them when they crossed the line into that danger zone. In retrospect, they may see that moment more clearly, as well as the turning point, the pivot that redirected them toward a return home. We can help them assess the costs and benefits of walking that path, and we can help them revisit the forks in that road, imagining alternative routes they could have selected—or created—and how they would handle similar situations in the future. One potential treasure resulting from any experience, positive or negative, is the wisdom gained from examining it in hindsight. At this point in the cycle, teenage heroes should look back and take stock; otherwise they may find themselves repeating a similar journey.

What was the worst choice you made as a teenager? You can see it now with perfect clarity, but did you realize where it would lead at the time? How long did it take for all the disruptions to resolve? Did you learn anything from that journey? Did those lessons stay with you and enable you to succeed in a later adventure?

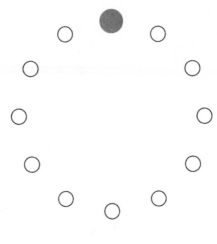

CHAPTER 12

Status Quo

H aving swept full circle, the cycle ends where it began: at twelve o'clock. Similar scenes at the start and end of a story often high-light what has changed and what has remained constant. Simba is raised above Pride Rock at the beginning of *The Lion King*, and an identical ceremony marks the end of that story, but now he sits on the throne and his child is being presented to his subjects. Each time Harry Potter returns to Privet Drive for the summer, the Dursleys treat him with a little more respect.

TWELVE O'CLOCK: **Colin at Home**

Colin drove up West Mombasha Road, cruising through the warm summer night and watching out for deer. He'd scrubbed himself clean of grime after a long kitchen shift, and his bristly hair dried in the breeze from the open window. This was his fifth summer working at the Tuxedo Club, and he'd risen from busboy to prep cook, making cold side dishes beside two culinary school-trained chefs in the club's

Golf House restaurant. He enjoyed watching his salads and sandwiches ride out on the waiters' trays beside the expertly prepared hot dishes. He was on friendly terms with most of the club's members, and they'd always been good to him, so it was strangely rewarding to feed them.

Tonight, during the dinner rush, he'd gotten a text from Ashley: "I'm not late anymore." He indulged in a silent fist pump before whipping together the next salad. He resisted the impulse to text back "told you" and instead sent a :) emoticon. "c u later @ Steve's," she wrote.

Now, as he turned left onto Fisher Lane, his headlights swept across more new houses. When he was a kid, this road was lined with summer bungalows like his own, but they had all been replaced by McMansions with three-car garages and walk-in closets. Colin had watched the slow gentrification from his school bus window each morning, curious to follow the construction from foundation to frame to finish. He wasn't sure if a single original house remained. One of these new houses belonged to Steve's family, and his parents were out of town.

Colin pulled into Steve's driveway, already crowded with cars. He spotted Ashley's Jetta. He walked around the garage toward music coming from the back deck. He recognized the tune as an Apex original—Steve's garage band with a few other friends. They played indie rock cover songs and also wrote their own music. Their tunes had an intimate, unproduced sound, and the one playing on the stereo was a slow ballad about packing for a long trip.

Colin rounded the corner and saw five people bouncing on the trampoline at the edge of the yard. Yelps peppered the air as the revelers bounced like popcorn. Three of them collided and collapsed in a heap of laughter. A handful of his friends were chatting on the low deck, sitting on chairs or on the railing. They held cigarettes or cans of Busch beer. Music flowed out the open sliding glass door from the homemade Apex CD playing inside.

"Colin!" Steve called his name, and everyone echoed. As Colin stepped onto the deck, he returned a few high-fives. Ashley slid through the group and wrapped her arms around Colin, greeting him with a kiss.

"Told you," Colin said.

"Shut. Up." Ashley whispered, smiling at him. "I'm going to talk to Claire."

As she walked away, Steve asked Colin, "Shot?" He held out a glass.

"Don't mind if I do," Colin said, tossing back a jigger of Absolut Mandarin. "Delicious."

"Hey, does Claire have a boyfriend?" Steve asked.

Colin considered for a moment. When Colin and Ashley had started dating, their distinct groups of friends started spending more time together at parties and small gatherings like this one. Claire was a rising senior, and Steve had just graduated. "I'm not sure. I don't think so."

Steve walked away, heading in her direction with his bottle and public shot glass.

Colin surveyed the crowd. Amet and Sanjay would be attending SUNY Binghamton in the fall, and three others would be at nearby Oneonta. They'd be four hours away from Clarkson, but they could easily get together once in a while. All his friends were getting excited to move away from home. They were working at the mall or doing landscaping to save up money. Colin remembered how that felt, the thrill of anticipation. Watching them now made him feel nostalgic and a little bit older.

Another Apex song played on the stereo. It was hard to make out the vocals, but Colin had heard the band play it dozens of times. Each verse described a different stage of life from childhood to old age, divided by the refrain "Looking back, I'm banging my head. So many things I should've said." It sometimes reminded Colin of that day at family court when Tim learned he had a son, the only time Colin had ever been in the same room with his biological father. He sometimes thought about what he would have said, if he'd known it was his only chance to talk to him. Sometimes it was a rant, sometimes a single word, and sometimes a scathing look.

But tonight the lyrics didn't remind him of that day. Looking across the yard at Ashley, he wished he'd had the guts to talk to her when he was still in high school. If he had just made some witty comment to her last year, they might have gotten together sooner. He watched her standing with such poise, the delicate angle of her neck, her fragile bones. It was still hard to believe she loved him.

"Colin!" Amet called.

Colin turned his head and caught the can of beer flying at him. Amet's smile followed close behind. "A toast!" he said, speaking over the music and raising his Busch. Colin popped the seal. "To good friends and good times!"

Colin met his friend's eyes, knowing his simple words contained their entire history—their backyard football games, the stink bomb incident, the prom, and everything in between. Colin nodded once, nodded again, and took a drink.

TWELVE O'CLOCK: **Cynthia on Track**

Cynthia's brain was about to melt. She leaned over the bubble sheet and test paper, struggling to process the last few questions of her Psychology exam. She had turned in her final project for Criminology last week, but today she had four final exams. She'd finished her Introduction to Criminal Justice test first thing in the morning, then American Legal Systems, then Sociology. She hadn't thought of finals when she'd arranged all her classes for Tuesdays and Thursdays.

She turned the page, and it was blank. No more questions. She checked her answer sheet to make sure she hadn't skipped any lines, then walked up to the teacher's desk.

"Finished?" Her teacher whispered, accepting her papers.

Cynthia nodded. She was the first one done.

He set them on the desk, face down, then stood up and shook Cynthia's hand. "Have a nice summer."

"You too," Cynthia said and walked outside.

It was already dark, with just a faint trace of the day remaining in the west. The summer heat hovered over the parking lot as Cynthia walked to her brother's car. He took classes on the same days she did, so they carpooled. She chirped the locks and slid into the passenger seat. The trapped heat rolled out around her as she turned the key counterclockwise and then lowered the windows.

Sitting there in the fog of mental exhaustion, Cynthia felt a ballast of certainty inside her, sort of like when she graduated high school. She looked back over the years since that day—her false starts at Pace, her bittersweet relationship with Paul, then moving back home. That visit from the DEA agents stuck with her. She'd never heard from them again, but her fear of them kept her honest. They might be watching her right now, for all she knew. Cynthia had stayed clean and stayed in school, and here she was now. Her fall courses hadn't meant very much—composition and math were a lot like high school—but this semester felt significant. Cynthia mentally tallied her probable scores on today's exams and concluded that her grades would be high enough to keep her on track for transfer into WestConn's four-year pre-law program.

She pressed the stereo power button and turned the volume up. Tiesto's "Magik Journey" started to play. A zephyr washed through the car's open windows as the low hum and dripping water introduced the song. A slow wave of strings came next, joined by a brass section and airy woodwinds. Two minutes into the song, the beat started— tinny and simple at first, gradually branching into multiple rhythms and tones. Cynthia bobbed her head, impatient for the drop. The bass pulsed and became more and more complex and industrial. This song was a tease, fading out to a background hiss and a solo voice, then skating back to the foreground with intense electronica, whipping melodies in circles, then softening for the singer again.

Cynthia heard the contrasting complexity and simplicity with different ears than when she had last heard the song. The lilting singer hit her high notes while everything else paused to listen, then the percussion beats whirled into motion again. She sang only a simple melody, no lyrics, but seemed trapped in a confusion of sound, trying to stabilize the storm with her gentle voice. Cynthia leaned the seat back and relaxed into the pulse of the subwoofer, floating through the rest of the tune, sure that she was ready for whatever came next.

TWELVE O'CLOCK: **Status Quo**

Stories typically end in a state of equilibrium after all the conflicts have been resolved. Twenty-three centuries ago, Aristotle wrote that all dramatic stories have a beginning, a middle, and an end. Two millennia later, we still anticipate that final resting point in a story's arc. This classical structure underlies the tale of Cinderella, which concludes with the heroine's wedding and the punishment of her treacherous stepsisters (they are blinded by pigeons in the Brothers Grimm version). Tolkien's final chapter of *The Lord of the Rings* trilogy chronicles two years of restored equilibrium, as Frodo recovers in the Shire before he, Bilbo, and Gandalf depart with the elves for the Grey Havens. Finally, ". . . the Third Age was over, and the Days of the Rings were passed, and an end was come of the story and song of those times."

Some modern stories offer a more unfinished ending, closing the final chapter soon after nine o'clock and before the cycle truly chimes twelve. For example, Alice and Dorothy have barely returned from their respective wonderlands when their stories end abruptly. *The Hunger Games* ends a few scenes later, while Katniss and Peeta are still en route to District 12 and her feelings remain unresolved. This unresolved tension propels the story forward into *Catching Fire*. Luke Skywalker and his friends receive their medals, but the credits roll before the story moves from Resolution to new Status Quo. Other stories tease the audience by sweeping quickly through the twelve o'clock hour to announce a new Call to Adventure. Think of the private eye or secret agent who solves the case and exchanges congratulations with his sidekick in the moment of relief—just before receiving an urgent message for the next mission, the sequel, another journey. Even stories that alter the monomyth formula still make use of it by playing against our expectations.

If you think of your favorite book or movie, it probably ends at or near a moment of stability. And that final resting point is, by definition, different from the situation rendered in the opening scene. Comparing the Status Quo at the end of the story to the Status Quo at the beginning reveals the impact of the story's events. How has the character changed? How has his or her world changed?

The same questions can be applied to our lives. Colin's journey lasted two decades, while Cynthia's took only a couple of years. The elastic monomyth formula can be adapted to journeys of any length: a road trip, a sports season, a nine-month school year, or a lifetime. Revisiting the personal example you provided in previous chapters, can you recall the moment when everything felt normal again? Now, compare that feeling to the equilibrium that existed before your journey began, before you heard the Call to Adventure. The two situations can't be identical. Even if the only difference is inside your mind, you completed a journey of sorts.

Of course this is so much simpler in fictional stories, where the main plot and all the subplots wind down at roughly the same time. In real life, we tend to pursue multiple goals simultaneously, juggling various quests in different stages. You may be teaching another year of school while coaching a sport, while pursuing a graduate degree. Maybe you're pregnant, and job hunting on top of all that. Theoretically, each of these adventures could be traced through twelve stages, beginning with the peaceful state beforehand, and ending with the peaceful state afterward. If you finish your sports season, the school year, and your graduate degree in the same month that you accept a job offer and bring home your new baby, then you can truly relax. But it's much more likely that your various quests will commence and conclude at offset moments.

The same applies to our teens. Challenges related to grades and sports will resolve according to a predictable schedule, but romances and friendships change direction without warning. Young people will find tranquility at the conclusion of a journey, but only within that single stratum of their deeply layered lives.

Coda

Colin

Colin and Ashley break up before he returns to Clarkson in August. During his sophomore year, Colin joins a fraternity. One afternoon his frat brothers are all splitting logs for a fire. Colin swings the ax like it's a baseball bat, and someone asks how come he never learned how to swing an ax properly. His best friend jokes, "What do you expect? He's got no dad." Colin laughs and lets everyone else in on the joke. Over time, each member acquires a nickname, which gets printed across the shoulders of his fraternity T-shirt. Colin's says NO DAD. Like Hercules, Colin has faced the lion, slain it, and now wears its hide as a trophy.

Colin is working at his first engineering job after college when a message appears on Facebook: "Do we have something in common?" It's from Colin's half-sister, Tim's daughter. They meet for lunch and spend hours getting to know each other, barely mentioning the man who abandoned them both. Sometime later, Colin notices a pop-up alert that their father, Tim, has become her friend on Facebook. Colin sends Tim a perfunctory message. "Thanks for the DNA. It's worked out real well for me." Tim never replies.

Colin rises within the engineering industry, specializing in designing and constructing municipal power plants. He takes on greater responsibilities, leads larger teams, and earns promotions within the top-ranked construction company in the United States. Throughout his hard work, Colin retains his impetuous sense of humor. On his job sites, everyone wears hardhats and sunglasses, so Colin cultivates a handlebar moustache for easy recognition. Around town, people react to it in different ways, and Colin enjoys upending their expectations, as always.

Cynthia

C ynthia passes all her exams that summer, then falls in love with a recovering heroin addict. Smitten, she moves in with him. He relapses, and she tries to help him quit. Instead of rescuing him, she ends up slipping into addiction alongside him. Her college dreams fall apart as her health deteriorates. She finally returns home to start over, one more time. Cynthia has repeated the same painful journey she just endured. Our fictional heroes triumph in the end, overcoming their enemies and their own weaknesses, but we flesh-and-blood mortals live beyond a single journey's auspicious finale, sometimes falling into patterns of behavior, good and bad. That never happens in myths, but it often happens in real life.

Thankfully, Cynthia survived the gruesome journey through heroin addiction. Then what? Did she ever complete her criminal justice degree, then her law degree, and then join a metropolitan public defender's office? No. In fact, she earned a medical qualification and found rewarding work in a nursing home, caring for the elderly. She continued to live at home, cultivating her relationship with her mom. She even adopted a puppy. Her life was moving in the right direction, slowly but surely.

One morning, Cynthia's mom realized she hadn't heard her daughter getting ready for work. She went upstairs to check on her, but Cynthia wouldn't wake up. Her skin was cold. Cynthia's mom checked for a pulse and found none. She called an ambulance and started CPR. The paramedics arrived and rushed Cynthia to the hospital, but it was too late. All those years of stimulants and depressants had taken their toll on Cynthia's heart. Now, when she had everything to live for, she had no life left. She passed away at the age of twenty-six.

Epilogue

The Hero's Journey formula offers an intuitively familiar framework for conversations with teens, but it has limitations. Real lives don't hinge on a single, high-stakes gambit, leading to a lifelong victory celebration, no matter what our books and movies suggest. Colin reconciled his inner conflict, but it remains a part of his identity. Cynthia survived a stormy journey, then set her sails for clear seas, but steered into a fresh tempest instead. After she'd finally reached still waters with fair weather, her life was unexpectedly cut short.

Do you know anyone who seems to repeat the same voyage? Perhaps a flawed lover who reruns the same, doomed relationship with each new partner? We can remain trapped within a pattern of behavior until we break that cycle. Joseph Campbell would point to the concept of reincarnation that permeates Eastern religions: Those who do not learn their lessons the first time around are doomed to revisit them in the next life. This concept also rings true through the repeating patterns within a single lifespan.

Campbell believed that a healthy human life comprises a series of heroic journeys, a continual orbit through that uncomfortable zone of exploration and discovery, then back through a period of equilibrium. However, these cycles should be progressive, not repetitive, like a planet stretching farther into unexplored space with each revolution. Each heroic cycle offers the chance to expand our understanding, to grow as a person, to develop more wisdom. Each new quest builds upon the last in a unique series of connected life lessons. After you close this book, you will surely open another.

Afterword

There is another Hero's Journey barely mentioned in these pages. Think back through all the stories we've touched on. Frodo Baggins, Luke and Anakin Skywalker, Katniss Everdeen. What about their mentors' stories? Gandalf fought the Balrog, died as the Gray, and returned as the White, vindicated in his faith in hobbit and human goodness. Obi-Wan Kenobi was tested and redeemed as surely as his young Padawan learners. Haymitch didn't fight in the same Hunger Games, but he facilitated Katniss's success in the arena while helping to orchestrate an uprising. Their stories are also transformative.

As mentors, we lay our hearts on the line too. Every coach sinks a whole lifetime of knowledge into his or her athletes at the start of each new sports season. Every teacher pushes a fresh crowd of students up this year's academic mountainside, realizing at the summit, *I learned something too.* Every preacher who shepherds a flock and every counselor who shines a light in dark places cannot help but be touched and expanded by those experiences. And every parent knows the transformative, bittersweet realization that accompanies each step of a child's journey toward adulthood.

I try to be mindful that each student has a private life, a confluence of forces that are driving the trajectory of his or her choices, and that the future chapters in each one's story will be determined, in part, by the choices he or she makes this week. My challenge is to be vigilant for clues about the crossroads my students face and what turn—right or wrong—they might take. It's easy to teach them how to pick the right pronoun, but choosing the right path requires deeper attention.

I wonder what Cynthia's story might have been if her beloved soccer coach had lived. It might be romantic to say that he stood between her and disaster, or it might be true. His simple presence in her life—expecting great things from her every afternoon—kept her more or less on the right path until she was sixteen. Had he coached her through high school and attended her games at Pace, would she have strayed so far from her potential success? It's impossible to know. None of us can measure the impact we have on the young people in our care; but with compassion and dedication, we can do our best to mentor them on their difficult and heroic journeys through adolescence.

• • •

Please visit mentoringteenageheroes.com where a thriving community of like-minded teachers, coaches, parents, counselors, and other mentors share stories and resources related to the hero's journey of adolescence.

Endnotes

1. Larsen, Stephen. *Joseph Campbell: A Fire in the Mind*. Rochester, Vermont: Inner Traditions. 2002. p. 541. And in Paley/Price Productions. "American Masters" *George Lucas: Heroes, Myths and Magic*. New York: Eagle Rock Entertainment. 1993.

2. Hamilton BE, Martin JA, Osterman MJK, et al. *Births: Final data for 2014. National vital statistics reports; vol 64 no 12*. Hyattsville, MD: National Center for Health Statistics. 2015. http://www.cdc.gov/nchs/fastats/unmarried-childbearing.htm

3. Tough, Paul. *How Children Succeed: Grit, Curiosity, and the Hidden Power of Character*. Boston: Houghton Mifflin Harcourt. 2012. p. 21.

4. Malory, Sir Thomas. *Le Morte d'Arthur*. Vol. II, Book XXI, Chapter IV. http://www.gutenberg.org/files/1252/1252-h/1252-h.htm#link 2HCH0256

5. Tolkien, J. R. R. *The Lord of the Rings*. New York: Houghton Mifflin Company, HarperCollins Publishers. 2005.

Bibliography

Aristotle. Trans. S. H. Butcher. *The Poetics of Aristotle*. Project Gutenberg: 2008. gutenberg.org/files/1974/1974-h/1974-h.htm

Baum, L. Frank. *The Wonderful Wizard of Oz*. Project Gutenberg: 2008. gutenberg.org/files/55/55-h/55-h.htm

Campbell, Joseph, and David Kudler. *Pathways to Bliss: Mythology and Personal Transformation*. Novato, California: New World Library, 2004. Print.

Campbell, Joseph. *Myths to Live By*. New York: Viking, 1972. Print.

Campbell, Joseph. *The Hero with a Thousand Faces*. Princeton, New Jersey: Princeton University Press, 1968. Print.

Carroll, Lewis. *Alice in Wonderland*. Project Gutenberg: 2006. gutenberg.org/files/19033/19033-h/19033-h.htm

Grimm, Jacob and Wilhelm. Trans. D. L. Ashliman. "Cinderella." University of Pittsburgh: 2011. pitt.edu/~dash/grimm021.html

Malory, Thomas. *Le Morte d'Arthur: The Book of King Arthur and of His Noble Knights of the Round Table*, Volume II. Project Gutenberg: 2009. gutenberg.org/files/1252/1252-h/1252-h.htm

Tolkien, J. R. R. *The Lord of the Rings*. New York: Houghton Mifflin Company, HarperCollins Publishers, 2005. Print.

Vogler, Christopher. *The Writer's Journey: Mythic Structure for Writers*. Studio City, California: Michael Wiese Productions, 2007. Print.

Acknowledgments

First, I'd like to thank everyone involved with my TED-Ed lesson, "What Makes a Hero?" especially Stephanie Lo, Director of TED-Ed Programs; Gerta Xhelo, who produced the lesson; along with award-winning video director Kirill Yeretsky (kirart.com) and his team at R/GA Digital Studios. "What Makes a Hero?" has been viewed millions of times on TED.com. That video, this book, and its companion website (mentoringteenageheroes.com) all grew out of my enrollment in Fairfield University's MFA program in Creative Writing. I must thank my many FUMFA friends who helped this manuscript evolve, most notably William B. Patrick and Eugenia Kim. Elizabeth Winkler and Laura Yerkovich also provided valuable feedback. My students and colleagues at South Kent School inspired this project; The Rectory School invited me to serve as Writer in Residence while I finished it; and my wife, Jessica, supported my devotion to it. Colin Hosten, David LeGere, Christopher Madden, and everyone at Woodhall Press believed in this book's potential and took a risk on this first-time author. I can't thank them enough. Finally, my deepest gratitude goes to Colin and Cynthia. Their brave confessions make *Mentoring Teenage Heroes* real, not imaginary, not theoretical. All of these contributions have coalesced into the book you now read, which would be pointless without you, dear reader. So I thank you, as well.

About the Author

Matthew P. Winkler has taught teenagers in middle schools, high schools, and colleges in New York, New England, China, and Japan. He lives in Connecticut where he is the Writer in Residence at The Rectory School. *Mentoring Teenage Heroes* is his debut book. Learn more at matthewpwinkler.com.